초등 영어 교재의 베스트셀러

초등 영어 문법 실력 쌓기!

Grammar Builder

1

Grammar Builder 1

©2015 by I am Books

지은이	이상건
펴낸이	신성현, 오상욱
영업관리	허윤정
펴낸곳	도서출판 아이엠북스
	153-802 서울시 금천구 가산디지털2로 14 1116 (대륭테크노타운 12차)
대표전화	02-6343-0999
팩스	02-6343-0995
출판등록	2006년 6월 7일
	제 313-2006-000122호
ISBN	978-89-6398-097-3 63740

www.iambooks.co.kr

초등 영어 교재의 베스트셀러

초등 영어 문법 실력 쌓기!

Grammar Builder

USA

You Are the Only One

1

Introduction   Grammar Builder는?

■ 이 책의 성격

문법 개념 설명부터 마무리 확인까지 실용 문제로 구성된 기본 영어 문법서

■ 이 책의 학습 목표 및 특징

- 다양하고 많은 문제를 통해 실전 문법을 익히고 영어 교과 과정을 대비한다.
- 이해하기 쉽게 설명한 문법의 개념과 원리를 바탕으로 문제를 통해 실력을 향상시킨다.
- 핵심 문법 개념을 이해하고 점진적으로 확장된 문제를 통해 문법 원리를 익힌다.
- 문법 학습뿐만 아니라 문장 패턴 학습과 기초 문장 영작을 통해 문장 쓰기를 훈련한다.
- 서술형 비중이 커지는 추세를 반영하여 학업 성취도 및 서술형 평가를 대비한다.

■ 이 책에 대한 세부 사항

- 문법 개념 설명부터 마무리 확인까지 문제 형식으로 구성하여 실전에 강하도록 하였다.
- 선택형 문제, 단답형 쓰기, 문장 패턴 쓰기로 확장하며 실력을 향상하도록 구성하였다.
- 단어와 문장을 정리하여 사전에 학습함으로 자연스럽게 문법 학습이 이루어지도록 하였다.
- 실전 문제와 서술형 문제를 강화하여 문법 개념과 원리를 응용할 수 있도록 하였다.

■ 이 책을 활용한 영어 문법 실력 쌓기

1. 문법 학습 전 정리된 단어와 문장을 먼저 예습한다.
    - 단어와 문장을 알면 어렵게 느껴지는 문법도 쉽게 학습할 수 있다.

2. 문법은 [이해＋암기]이다. 필요한 문법 사항은 암기한다.
    - 문법의 쓰임과 역할을 이해하고 암기하여 필요할 때 적용하는 것이 좋다.

3. 문법을 학습할 때 예문을 통해 문법 개념을 학습한다.
    - 예문을 문법적으로 파악하면 문장이 복잡해도 쉽게 이해할 수 있다.

4. 문제를 푸는 것으로 끝내지 않고 대화나 글로 마무리한다.
    - 문법을 배우는 이유는 글을 이해하고 쓸 수 있는 능력을 갖추기 위한 것이다.

Grammar Series Contents

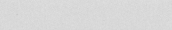

contents

About This Book 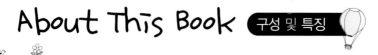 구성 및 특징

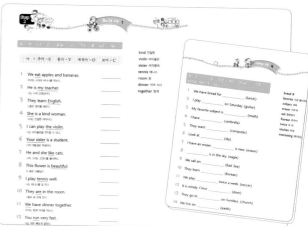

1. Unit별 핵심 문법 개념 정리

Unit별 학습 목표를 제시하여 중점 사항을 파악하도록 하였고, 기초적인 문법 사항을 쉽게 이해할 수 있도록 설명하여 문법 개념 이해를 돕습니다. 또한 다양한 예문을 통해 문법 원리 학습을 적용하여 이해하도록 하였습니다.

2. Step 1 – Check Up

학습 목표와 핵심 문법 개념에 대한 기초적인 확인 문제로 구성하여 문법 원리를 문제를 통해서 익히도록 하였습니다. 스스로 풀어보면서 반복 학습을 통해 문법의 규칙을 이해하도록 하였습니다.

3. Step 2 – Build Up

다양한 형식의 다소 난이도 있는 문제로 구성하여 앞에서 배운 내용을 반복, 복습하며 문법 원리를 익히도록 하였습니다. 학습한 내용을 본격적으로 적용하고 응용해 보면서 다양한 유형을 연습하도록 하였습니다.

4. Step 3 – Jump Up

핵심 문법 개념을 스스로 정리해 보도록 하여 이해도를 확인하고 보완하도록 하였으며 확장형 응용문제를 통해 학습 목표를 성취하도록 하였습니다. 또한 영작문 실력이 향상되도록 서술형 문제 위주로 구성하였습니다.

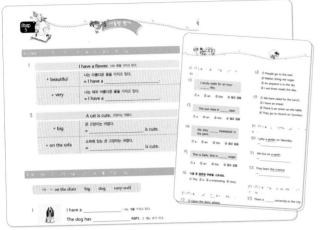

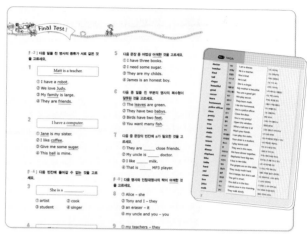

5. Step 4 – 실전 평가

Unit별 핵심 문법 개념과 다양한 문제로 익힌 문법 사항을 마무리 테스트로 구성하여 스스로 점검해 보도록 하였습니다. 이를 통해 문법 문제에 대한 응용력을 키우고 시험 유형에 대비하도록 하였습니다.

6. Step 5 – 서술평 평가

점점 서술형 비중이 커지는 추세를 반영하여 영작문 위주로 구성된 Unit별 종합 문제를 풀어보면서 Unit을 정리하고 학업성취도 평가 및 서술형 평가를 대비하도록 히였습니다.

7. Final Test

본 교재를 통해서 배운 핵심 문법 개념과 문법 사항을 종합평가로 풀어보면서 정리하고 마무리하도록 하였습니다. 종합적으로 배운 내용을 확인하고 점검하도록 하였습니다.

8. Words in Grammar

본 교재의 본문에 사용된 단어들과 문장을 정리하여 문법 학습에 활용하도록 하였습니다. 예습으로 단어를 학습하고 학습 집중도를 올리도록 활용하는 것이 좋습니다.

Curriculum

Book	Month	Week	Hour	Unit	
1	1	1	1	1. 문장의 기본 구성	Words 활용
			2		서술형 평가
		2	1	2. 셀 수 있는 명사	Words 활용
			2		서술형 평가
		3	1	3. 셀 수 없는 명사	Words 활용
			2		서술형 평가
		4	1	4. 관사	Words 활용
			2		서술형 평가
	2	1	1	5. 인칭대명사와 격변화	Words 활용
			2		서술형 평가
		2	1	6. 지시대명사, 지시형용사	Words 활용
			2		서술형 평가
		3	1	7. be동사의 현재시제	Words 활용
			2		서술형 평가
		4	1	8. be동사의 부정문, 의문문	Words 활용
			2		서술형 평가
2	3	1	1	1. 일반동사의 현재시제	Words 활용
			2		서술형 평가
		2	1	2. 일반동사의 부정문, 의문문	Words 활용
			2		서술형 평가
		3	1	3. There is/are, 비인칭주어 it	Words 활용
			2		서술형 평가
		4	1	4. 형용사	Words 활용
			2		서술형 평가
	4	1	1	5. Some, Any, All, Every	Words 활용
			2		서술형 평가
		2	1	6. 수량형용사	Words 활용
			2		서술형 평가
		3	1	7. 부사	Words 활용
			2		서술형 평가
		4	1	8. 현재진행형	Words 활용
			2		서술형 평가
3	5	1	1	1. 기수와 서수	Words 활용
			2		서술형 평가
		2	1	2. 부정대명사, 재귀대명사	Words 활용
			2		서술형 평가
		3	1	3. 비교 구문	Words 활용
			2		서술형 평가
		4	1	4. 조동사	Words 활용
			2		서술형 평가

Grammar Builder 시리즈는 총 5권으로 구성되어 있으며, 권당 8주(2개월) 16차시(Unit당 2차시 수업)로 학습할 수 있도록 구성하였습니다. 주 2회 수업을 기준으로 하였으며 학습자와 학습 시간에 따라 변경이 가능합니다.

Book	Month	Week	Hour	Unit	
3	6	1	1	5. 동사의 과거시제	Words 활용
			2		서술형 평가
		2	1	6. 과거시제의 부정문, 의문문	Words 활용
			2		서술형 평가
		3	1	7. 과거진행형	Words 활용
			2		서술형 평가
		4	1	8. 동사의 미래시제	Words 활용
			2		서술형 평가
4	7	1	1	1. 의문사 의문문	Words 활용
			2		서술형 평가
		2	1	2. 의문대명사와 의문형용사	Words 활용
			2		서술형 평가
		3	1	3. 의문부사	Words 활용
			2		서술형 평가
		4	1	4. 명령문	Words 활용
			2		서술형 평가
	8	1	1	5. 감탄문	Words 활용
			2		서술형 평가
		2	1	6. 접속사	Words 활용
			2		서술형 평가
		3	1	7. 전치사	Words 활용
			2		서술형 평가
		4	1	8. 부정의문문, 부가의문문	Words 활용
			2		서술형 평가
5	9	1	1	1. to부정사	Words 활용
			2		서술형 평가
		2	1	2. 동명사	Words 활용
			2		서술형 평가
		3	1	3. 현재분사와 과거분사	Words 활용
			2		서술형 평가
		4	1	4. 문장의 형식 1	Words 활용
			2		서술형 평가
	10	1	1	5. 문장의 형식 2	Words 활용
			2		서술형 평가
		2	1	6. 현재완료	Words 활용
			2		서술형 평가
		3	1	7. 수동태	Words 활용
			2		서술형 평가
		4	1	8. 관계대명사	Words 활용
			2		서술형 평가

❀ 발음 기호를 익혀보세요.

I. 모음: 주로 a, e, i, o, u의 철자에서 나는 소리로 모두 유성음이다.

æ apple [ǽpl]
'애'처럼 발음하되 입을 좀 더 크게 벌린다.

e desk [desk]
'에'처럼 발음하되 입을 양 옆으로 좀 더 넓게 벌린다.

i fish [fiʃ]
'에'에 가깝게 '이'를 발음한다.

iː meat [miːt]
[i]를 길게 발음한다.

ɑ octopus [ɑ́ktəpəs]
'아' 보다 조금 강하게 발음한다.

ɑː car [kɑːr]
[ɑ]를 길게 발음한다.

u foot [fut]
'우'와 '으'의 중간 정도로 발음한다.

uː food [fuːd]
[u]를 길게 발음한다.

ə banana [bənǽnə]
'어' 보다 약하게 발음한다. 강세가 오지 않는 모음이다.

əː bird [bəːrd]
[ə]를 길게 발음한다.

ɔ doll [dɑːl]
'오' 보다 턱을 좀 더 아래로 내리고 발음한다.

ɔː ball [bɔːl]
턱을 내리고 입 천장은 높여서 입 안에 공간을 크게 하여 발음한다.

ʌ umbrella [ʌmbrélə]
입모양은 '어' 보다 좀 더 벌리고 '어'와 '아'의 중간 정도로 발음한다.

ɛə bear [bɛər]
'에어'로 발음한다.

ei baby [béibi]
'에이'로 발음하되 '에'는 강하게 '이'는 약하고 짧게 발음한다.

ai eye [ai]
'아이'로 발름하되 '아'는 강하게 '이'는 약하고 짧게 발음한다.

au cow [kau]
'아우'로 발음하되 '아'는 강하게 '우'는 약하고 짧게 발음한다.

ou window [wíndou]
'오우'로 발음하되 '오'는 강하게 '우'는 약하고 짧게 발음한다.

2. 반모음: 혼자서는 소리가 나지 않고 모음과 합쳐져서만 소리가 난다.

j yacht [jɑːt]
'이'와 '으'의 중간 소리 정도로 약하게 발음한다.

w water [wɔ́ːtər]
'우'와 '어'의 중간 소리 정도로 약하게 발음한다.

12

3. 자음: 성대를 울리는 유성음과 성대를 울리지 않는 무성음이 있다.

p pencil [pénsəl]
'프'과 비슷하게 발음한다.

b book [buk]
'q'와 비슷하나 성대를 울리는 유성음이다.

f fruit [fruːt]
윗니가 아랫입술을 스치면서 '프'과 비슷하게 발음한다.

v violin [vàiəlín]
[f]처럼 윗니가 아랫입술을 스치면서 발음하지만 유성음이다.

t tent [tent]
'트'과 비슷하게 발음한다.

d doctor [dáːktər]
'ㄷ'과 비슷하게 발음하지만 성대를 울리는 유성음이다.

k cake [keik]
'ㅋ'과 비슷하게 발음한다.

g glove [glʌv]
'ㄱ'과 비슷하게 발음하지만 성대를 울리는 유성음이다.

s soccer [sákər]
'ㅅ'보다 강하게 발음한다.

z zoo [zuː]
'ㅈ'과 비슷하게 발음하지만 성대를 울리는 유성음이다.

θ doll [dɑːl]
'오'보다 턱을 좀 더 아래로 내리고 발음한다.

ɔː ball [bɔːl]
턱을 내리고 입 천장은 높여서 입 안에 공간을 크게 하여 발음한다.

ʃ shoes [ʃuːz]
'쉬'와 비슷하게 발음한다.

ʒ television [téləvìʒən]
[ʃ]와 비슷한 입모양을 한 상태에서 성대를 울리며 발음한다.

tʃ church [tʃəːrtʃ]
'취'와 비슷하게 발음한다.

dʒ danger [déindʒər]
'쥐'와 비슷하게 발음한다.

m mouse [maus]
'ㅁ'과 비슷하게 발음한다.

n nail [neil]
'ㄴ'과 비슷하게 발음한다.

l lake [leik]
'ㄹ'과 비슷하게 발음한다.

r rocket [rɑːkit]
'l'와 비슷하지만 입천장에 혀끝이 닿지 않게 혀끝을 구부리고 발음한다.

h horse [hɔːrs]
'ㅎ'과 비슷하게 발음한다.

ŋ song [suŋ]
우리말의 받침 'ㅇ'과 비슷하게 발음한다.

문장의 기본 구성

영어의 8품사를 이해하고 활용할 수 있다.

문장의 특성과 문장 구성 요소를 이해할 수 있다.

문장의 종류를 구분할 수 있다.

문장은 단어로 이루어져 있는데, 문장이 집이라면 단어는 집을 짓는 지붕, 기둥, 벽돌 등이라고 할 수 있어요. 우리 눈에 보이게 나눠지는 하나 하나를 단어라고 하고, 이들이 모여서 마침표(.), 물음표(?), 느낌표(!) 등으로 끝나는 것을 문장이라고 해요. 또한 이러한 문장을 구성하기 위해서는 문장에서 주어, 동사, 목적어, 보어 등 단어의 역할이 필요해요.

Unit 1 문장의 기본 구성

1. 단어와 문장

단어는 문장을 구성하는 작은 단위로 단어들이 모여서 문장이 된다. 문장이 집이라면 단어는 집을 이루는 지붕, 기둥, 벽돌이라고 할 수 있다.

I   study   English.
단어 + 단어 + 단어 = 문장

2. 문장의 구성 요소

여러 개의 단어들이 일정한 규칙에 따라 나열되어 하나의 의미를 나타내는 것을 문장이라고 한다.

[문장 ×] flowers 꽃들 I flowers 나 꽃들 flowers like 꽃들 좋아한다

[문장 O] I like flowers. 나는 꽃들을 좋아한다.

• 문장의 특성

❶ 명령문을 제외한 모든 문장에서는 주어와 동사가 있어야 한다.

❷ 첫 글자는 항상 대문자로 시작한다.

❸ 문장 끝에는 마침표, 느낌표, 물음표와 같은 문장 부호를 쓴다.

❹ 주어, 동사, 목적어, 보어 등 단어의 역할이 필요하다.

(1) 주어, 동사

• 주어: 동사의 주체가 되는 말로 '~은/는, ~이/가'로 해석한다. 주어는 문장의 맨 앞에 나오며 주로 명사나 대명사가 주어로 쓰인다.

- 동사: 주어의 상태나 동작을 나타내는 말로 '~이다, ~하다'로 해석한다. 일반적으로 동사는 주어 다음에 온다.

The woman is a doctor. 그 여자는 의사이다.
   주어   동사

They eat apples. 그들은 사과를 먹는다.
  주어 동사

(2) 목적어, 보어, 수식어

- 목적어: 동작의 대상이 되는 말로 동사 뒤에 오며 '~을/를'로 해석한다.

We eat hamburgers for lunch. 우리는 점심으로 햄버거를 먹는다.

We study English. 우리는 영어를 공부한다.

- 보어: 동사 뒤에 쓰여 주어의 상태나 성질을 설명하는 말로 명사나 형용사가 보어로 쓰인다.

He is my father. 그는 나의 아버지다. [명사 보어]

She is kind. 그녀는 친절하다. [형용사 보어]

- 수식어: 다른 말을 꾸며주는 말로 형용사나 부사가 수식어로 쓰인다.

She is a kind teacher. 그녀는 친절한 선생님이다.

> **Pop Quiz**   **I.** 다음 문장에서 주어에 ○표, 동사에 △표 하세요.
>   ❶ We are students.   ❷ They play soccer.

3. 문장의 종류

영어 문장은 형태와 의미에 따라서 4가지로 나눌 수 있다.

(1) 평서문: 사실을 서술하는 문장으로 문장 끝에 마침표를 찍으며, '~은 …이다'라는 긍정문과 '~은 …이 아니다'라는 부정문이 있다.

She is a nurse. 그녀는 간호사이다.

He is not a teacher. 그는 선생님이 아니다.

(2) 의문문: 상대방에게 무언가를 묻는 문장으로 마지막에 물음표를 붙인다.

Is he a teacher? 그는 선생님이니?

(3) 명령문: 상대방에게 지시하거나 명령하는 문장으로 동사로 시작한다.

Open the window. 창문을 열어라.

(4) 감탄문: 놀람이나 감탄을 나타내는 문장으로 마지막에 느낌표를 붙인다.

She is very tall!(How tall she is!) 그녀는 키가 무척 크구나!

What a pretty girl she is! 그녀는 정말 예쁜 소녀구나!

> **Pop Quiz**
>
> **2.** 다음 문장의 종류를 쓰세요.(평서문이면 '평'을, 의문문이면 '의'를, 명령문이면 '명'을, 감탄문이면 '감'을 쓰세요.)
>
> ❶ I am a teacher. (　　) ❷ Close the door. (　　)
>
> ❸ Is she a nurse? (　　) ❹ What a cute girl she is! (　　)

4. 영어의 8품사

성질이나 문법적 역할이 같은 단어끼리 모아 놓은 것을 품사라고 하는데, 영어에서는 8개의 품사로 구분할 수 있다.

(1) 이름 名 명사: 사람, 동물, 사물이나 장소뿐만 아니라 눈에 보이지 않는 것들의 이름도 나타낸다. 문장에서는 주어, 목적어, 보어로 쓰인다.

- 사람: teacher 선생님, girl 소녀, Tom 탐, Ann 앤
- 동물: cat 고양이, dog 개, tiger 호랑이, lion 사자

- 사물: chair 의자, desk 책상, cup 컵, telephone 전화기
- 장소: house 집, hospital 병원, school 학교, Seoul 서울
- 눈에 보이지 않는 것: time 시간, love 사랑, peace 평화

(2) 대신 代 대명사: 사람이나 사물의 이름을 대신하는 말로, 문장에서 주어, 목적어, 보어로 쓰인다.

- 인칭대명사: 사람이나 동물, 사물을 대신하여 나타내는 말
  ▶ I 나, you 너, he 그, she 그녀, it 그것, we 우리, they 그들/그것들

- 지시대명사: '이것' 또는 '저것'이라고 대상을 가리키는 말
  ▶ this 이것, that 저것, these 이것들, those 저것들

(3) 움직일 動 동사: 사람이나 동물, 사물의 동작이나 상태를 나타내는 말이다. 모든 문장에는 반드시 동사가 필요하다.

- be동사: '~이다, ~이 있다'라는 뜻으로 am, are, is 등이 있다.

- 일반동사: 동작이나 상태를 나타내는 대부분의 동사
  ▶ go 가다, eat 먹다, make 만들다, study 공부하다, run 달리다

- 조동사: be동사나 일반동사 앞에서 동사의 뜻을 더하는 역할을 한다.
  ▶ can ~할 수 있다, will ~할 것이다, must ~해야 한다

(4) 모양 形 형용사: 사람이나 사물의 성질, 성격, 상태 등을 나타내는 말이다. 명사 앞에서 명사를 꾸며주는 역할을 하고, 동사 뒤에서 사람이나 사물의 상태를 설명해 주는 역할을 한다.

  ▶ big 큰, small 작은, tall 키가 큰, beautiful 아름다운, cute 귀여운

- 명사 앞:

a beautiful flower   a tall boy   a cute baby
아름다운 꽃   키가 큰 소년   귀여운 아기

• 동사 뒤: He is happy. 그는 행복하다.

(5) 덧붙일 副 부사: 방법, 정도 등을 나타내며 동사, 형용사, 부사 또는 문장 전체를 꾸며 주는 말이다.

▶ very 매우, really 정말로, late 늦게, early 일찍, well 잘

I play the piano well. 나는 피아노를 잘 연주한다.

(6) 앞 前 전치사: 명사나 대명사 앞에 쓰이며 장소, 시간, 목적, 수단 등을 나타내는 말이다. 〈전치사+명사〉로 문장에서 수식어로 쓰인다.

▶ in ~ 안에, on ~ 위에, under ~ 아래에, with ~와 함께, to ~로

| in the box | on the table | under the chair |
| 상자 안에 | 탁자 위에 | 의자 아래에 |

(7) 이을 接 접속사: 단어와 단어, 구와 구, 절과 절을 이어주는 말이다.

▶ and 그리고(~와), but 그러나, so 그래서

Tom and Kate are students. Tom과 Kate는 학생들이다.

(8) 느낄 感 감탄사: 기쁨, 슬픔, 놀람 등의 감정을 나타내는 말이다.

▶ Oh! 오!, Wow! 와우!, Ouch! 아이쿠!, Oops! 저런!

Pop Quiz **3.** 다음 중 같은 품사가 <u>아닌</u> 것에 동그라미 하세요.

❶ eat make book　　❷ small cute very

다음을 단어와 문장으로 구별하여 빈칸에 쓰세요.

flower   He is not a teacher.   are   dog   tall
he   English   He is tall.   door   She is kind.
I am a doctor.   woman   doctor   father   teacher

woman 여자
doctor 의사
teacher 선생님
tall 키가 큰
door 문

1 단어

_____   _____   _____

_____   _____   _____

_____   _____   _____

_____   _____

2 문장

_____

_____

_____

_____

다음 문장에서 주어에는 ○표, 동사에는 △표 하세요.

1	They eat apples.	그들은 사과를 먹는다.
2	She is a singer.	그녀는 가수이다.
3	We play the piano.	우리는 피아노를 연주한다.
4	They like flowers.	그들은 꽃을 좋아한다.
5	My mother is beautiful.	나의 어머니는 아름답다.
6	You are a good girl.	너는 착한 소녀이다.

singer 가수
beautiful 아름다운
good 착한, 좋은
soccer 축구
learn 배우다
math 수학
homework 숙제

다음 문장에서 목적어에는 ○표, 보어에는 △표 하세요.

7	He is my father.	그는 나의 아버지이다.
8	We play soccer.	우리는 축구를 한다.
9	Your dog is cute.	너의 개는 귀엽다.
10	They learn math.	그들은 수학을 배운다.
11	This cat is big.	이 고양이는 크다.
12	I do the homework.	나는 숙제를 한다.

다음 〈보기〉를 참고하여 문장의 종류를 쓰세요.

〈보기〉 평서문   의문문   명령문   감탄문

1   He is a police officer. 그는 경찰관이다.   _____

2   Close the door. 문을 닫아라.   _____

3   She is very pretty! 그녀는 무척 예쁘구나!   _____

4   She is not a doctor. 그녀는 의사가 아니다.   _____

5   Are you a singer? 너는 가수니?   _____

6   How tall he is! 그는 정말 키가 크구나!   _____

7   Open the window. 창문을 열어라.   _____

8   They are students. 그들은 학생들이다.   _____

9   Is this your book? 이것은 너의 책이니?   _____

10   What a tall tree it is! 그것은 정말 큰 나무구나!   _____

11   Wash your hands. 너의 손을 씻어라.   _____

12   Is he a teacher? 그는 선생님이니?   _____

police officer
경찰관
close 닫다
pretty 예쁜
open 열다
book 책
tree 나무
wash 씻다

다음 단어들에 해당하는 품사를 〈보기〉에서 골라 쓰세요.

〈보기〉	명사	대명사	동사	형용사
	부사	접속사	전치사	감탄사

small 작은
but 그러나
school 학교
for ~를 위해
make 만들다
late 늦게
early 일찍

1 big, small, pretty, cute, good, tall　_____

2 I, you, he, they, we, this, that　_____

3 and, but, so　_____

4 chair, school, time, love, Tom, lion　_____

5 in, on, under, with, to, for　_____

6 oh, wow, ouch, oops　_____

7 go, eat, make, study, run, have　_____

8 very, really, late, early, well　_____

다음 〈보기〉를 참고하여 문장에서 밑줄 친 말의 구성 요소를 쓰세요.

kind	친절한
violin	바이올린
sister	여자 형제
tennis	테니스
room	방
dinner	저녁 식사
together	함께

〈보기〉 주어 – S   동사 – V   목적어 – O   보어 – C

1 We <u>eat</u> apples and bananas.   _____
우리는 사과들과 바나나들을 먹는다.

2 He is <u>my teacher</u>.   _____
그는 나의 선생님이다.

3 They learn <u>English</u>.   _____
그들은 영어를 배운다.

4 She is <u>a kind woman</u>.   _____
그녀는 친절한 여자이다.

5 I can play <u>the violin</u>.   _____
나는 바이올린을 연주할 수 있다.

6 <u>Your sister</u> is a student.   _____
너의 여동생은 학생이다.

7 He and she <u>like</u> cats.   _____
그와 그녀는 고양이를 좋아한다.

8 This flower is <u>beautiful</u>.   _____
이 꽃은 아름답다.

9 I play <u>tennis</u> well.   _____
나는 테니스를 잘 친다.

10 They <u>are</u> in the room.   _____
그들은 방 안에 있다.

11 We have <u>dinner</u> together.   _____
우리는 함께 저녁을 먹는다.

12 <u>You</u> run very fast.   _____
너는 매우 빠르게 달린다.

다음 〈보기〉를 참고하여 알맞은 품사를 고르세요.

elephant 코끼리
ear 귀
bike 자전거
table 탁자
hard 열심히
happy 행복한
sad 슬픈

〈보기〉	명사 – 명　대명사 – 대　형용사 – 형　부사 – 부
	동사 – 동　전치사 – 전　감탄사 – 감　접속사 – 접

1 We are teachers. 우리는 선생님들이다.
(명/대) (동/접) (명/형)

2 Elephants have big ears. 코끼리는 큰 귀를 가지고 있다.
(대/명) (동/부) (형/부) (감/명)

3 I buy a new bike. 나는 새 자전거를 산다.
(동/형) (전/형) (명/동)

4 Oops! I am sorry. 이런! 미안해.
(대/감) (동/대) (부/형)

5 The baby is on the bed. 그 아기는 침대 위에 있다.
(동/부) (접/전) (명/대)

6 Jane and Kate are very tall. Jane과 Kate는 아주 키가 크다.
(대/명) (접/감) (부/형) (형/대)

7 They study math hard. 그들은 수학을 열심히 공부한다.
(대/동) (명/형) (부/전)

8 The grapes are on the table. 그 포도는 탁자 위에 있다.
(명/형) (동/접) (전/명)

9 We like dogs and cats. 우리는 개와 고양이를 좋아한다.
(명/대) (동/부) (접/전) (전/명)

10 He is happy, but she is sad. 그는 행복하지만, 그녀는 슬프다.
(명/대) (형/부) (전/접) (동/명)

다음 〈보기〉를 참고하여 문장에서 밑줄 친 단어의 품사를 쓰세요.

〈보기〉	명사	대명사	형용사	부사
	동사	전치사	감탄사	접속사

smart 영리한
box 상자
juice 주스
walk 걷다
slowly 천천히

1 You <u>are</u> a boy.   _____
너는 소년이다.

2 <u>We</u> play the piano well.   _____
우리는 피아노를 잘 친다.

3 The girl is <u>smart</u>.   _____
그 소녀는 영리하다.

4 She is a <u>singer</u>.   _____
그녀는 가수이다.

5 The <u>doll</u> is in the box.   _____
그 인형은 그 상자 안에 있다.

6 This cat is <u>very</u> cute.   _____
이 고양이는 매우 귀엽다.

7 That <u>room</u> is small.   _____
저 방은 작다.

8 I <u>drink</u> juice in the morning.   _____
나는 아침에 주스를 마신다.

9 They walk <u>slowly</u>.   _____
그들은 천천히 걷는다.

10 The man <u>and</u> woman are doctors.   _____
그 남자와 여자는 의사이다.

11 I play <u>with</u> my friends.   _____
나는 나의 친구들과 함께 논다.

12 <u>Wow</u>! It is very good.   _____
와우! 그것은 매우 좋다.

다음 빈칸에 알맞은 말을 쓰세요.

1 단어들이 규칙에 따라 나열되어 하나의 의미를 나타내는 것을 _____이라고 한다.

〈규칙〉 **1.** 명령문을 제외한 모든 문장에서는 주어와 _____가 있어야 한다. **2.** 첫 글자는 항상 _____
로 시작한다. **3.** 문장 끝에는 _____, 느낌표, 물음표와 같은 문장 부호를 쓴다. **4.** 주어, 동사, _____,
_____ 등 단어의 역할이 필요하다.

2 문장의 종류는 형태와 의미에 따라서 4가지로 나눌 수 있다. 문장의 4가지 종류에는 _____, 의문문,
_____, 감탄문이 있다.

3 성질이나 문법적 역할이 같은 _____끼리 모아 놓은 것을 _____라고 하는데, 영어에서는 _____개
의 품사로 구분할 수 있다.

_____	세상에 있는 모든 것들의 이름을 나타내는 말이다. 문장에서 주어, 목적어, 보어로 쓰인다.
대명사	사람이나 사물의 이름을 대신하는 말이다.
_____	동작이나 상태를 나타내는 말로 모든 문장에서는 반드시 필요하다.
_____	사람이나 사물의 성질, 성격, 상태 등을 나타내는 말이다.
부사	방법, 정도 등을 나타내며 _____, _____, _____ 또는 문장 전체를 꾸며 주는 말이다.
전치사	_____나 _____ 앞에 쓰이며 장소, _____, 목적, 수단 등을 나타내는 말이다.
_____	단어와 단어, 구와 구, 절과 절을 이어주는 말이다.
_____	기쁨, 슬픔, 놀람 등의 _____을 나타내는 말이다.

다음 〈보기〉를 참고하여 알맞은 품사를 쓰세요.

horse 말
carrot 당근
sofa 소파
friend 친구
morning 아침
play 연주하다
sleep 자다

〈보기〉
명사 – 명   대명사 – 대   형용사 – 형   부사 – 부
동사 – 동   전치사 – 전   감탄사 – 감   접속사 – 접

1 The horse likes carrots. 말은 당근을 좋아한다.
(   ) (   ) (   )

2 He is on the chair. 그는 그 의자에 앉아 있다.
(   ) (   ) (   )   (   )

3 Wow! The flower is very beautiful. 와우! 그 꽃은 매우 아름답다.
(   )   (   ) (   )(   ) (   )

4 I like apples but Ann likes oranges.
(   ) (   ) (   ) (   ) (   )

나는 사과를 좋아하지만 Ann은 오렌지를 좋아한다.

5 The cute cat is on the sofa. 그 귀여운 고양이는 소파 위에 있다.
(   ) (   ) (   )(   ) (   )

6 Jane and you are good friends. Jane과 너는 좋은 친구들이다.
(   ) (   ) (   ) (   ) (   ) (   )

7 We drink milk in the morning. 우리는 아침에 우유를 마신다.
(   ) (   ) (   ) (   )   (   )

8 The dog has big ears. 그 개는 귀가 크다.
(   ) (   ) (   ) (   )

9 She plays the piano very well. 그녀는 피아노를 아주 잘 친다.
(   ) (   )   (   ) (   ) (   )

10 The baby sleeps on the bed. 그 아기는 침대에서 잔다.
(   ) (   ) (   )   (   )

1 다음 중 완전한 문장을 고르세요.

① My dog cute

② a beautiful flower

③ He is a teacher.

④ is on the chair.

[2~3] 다음 중 잘못된 문장을 고르세요.

2 ① they eat apples.

② She is a nurse.

③ Open the window.

④ How tall he is!

3 ① We play the piano.

② Are you a student.

③ This is very big!

④ I study English.

[4~5] 다음 중 문장의 종류가 다른 것을 고르세요.

4 ① They like flowers.

② Close the door.

③ He is my father.

④ We play soccer.

5 ① What a pretty girl she is!

② Ann is beautiful.

③ My cat is very cute.

④ You are a good boy.

6 다음 중 밑줄 친 부분의 역할이 다른 것을 고르세요.

① I eat sandwiches for lunch.

② They like bananas.

③ She is my mother.

④ We learn math.

[7~9] 다음 중 같은 품사의 단어끼리 짝지어진 것을 고르세요.

7 ① small – under

② teacher – he

③ tiger – hospital

④ eat – and

8 ① Seoul – can

② make – study

③ oops – cute

④ late – but

9 ① really – early

② love – with

③ beautiful – we

④ they – have

[10~12] 다음 중 밑줄 친 부분의 품사가 다른 것을 고르세요.

10 ① He loves his mom.
　　② Kate is so pretty.
　　③ This is my eraser.
　　④ We are doctors.

11 ① We play soccer well.
　　② They run slowly.
　　③ She studies English hard.
　　④ He goes to the library.

12 ① I buy a new bike.
　　② That is a table.
　　③ Elephants are big.
　　④ It is very tall.

[13~14] 다음 우리말과 같도록 괄호 안에서 알맞은 것에 동그라미 하세요.

13 Tom과 Kate는 학생들이다.
　　→ Tom (and, but) Kate are students.

14 그 고양이는 의자 아래에 있다.
　　→ The cat is (on, under) the chair.

[15~16] 다음 문장에서 주어에는 ○표, 동사에는 △표 하세요.

15 They play the piano well.

16 This is very pretty.

[17~18] 다음 문장에서 목적어에는 ○표, 보어에는 △표 하세요.

17 She is a teacher.

18 I drink milk every day.

[19~20] 다음 문장에서 틀린 부분을 찾아 바르게 고쳐 다시 쓰세요.

19 the man is a doctor
　　→ _____

20 Are you a good student.
　　→ _____

A 우리말과 같은 뜻이 되도록 주어진 말을 넣어 문장을 다시 쓰세요.

1

I have a flower. 나는 꽃을 가지고 있다.

| + beautiful | 나는 아름다운 꽃을 가지고 있다.
= I have a _____. |
| + very | 나는 매우 아름다운 꽃을 가지고 있다.
= I have a _____. |

2

A cat is cute. 고양이는 귀엽다.

| + big | 큰 고양이는 귀엽다.
= _____ is cute. |
| + on the sofa | 소파에 있는 큰 고양이는 귀엽다.
= _____ is cute. |

B 다음 그림을 보고, 〈보기〉에서 알맞은 말을 골라 빈칸에 쓰세요.

〈보기〉 on the chair   big   dog   very well

1 I have a _____. 나는 개를 가지고 있다.

The dog has _____ ears. 그 개는 귀가 크다.

2 She is _____. 그녀는 의자에 앉아 있다.

She plays the piano _____. 그녀는 피아노를 아주 잘 친다.

셀 수 있는 명사

셀 수 있는 명사에는 어떤 것들이 있는지 이해할 수 있다.

셀 수 있는 명사의 복수형을 알고 활용할 수 있다.

세상에 있는 것들은 모두 이름을 가지고 있어요. 사람이나 동물, 사물, 장소 등 세상에 있는 모든 것들의 이름을 나타내는 말을 명사라고 해요. 명사는 셀 수 있는 명사와 셀 수 없는 명사가 있는데, 셀 수 있는 명사와 셀 수 없는 명사를 구분하고 셀 수 있는 명사의 복수형을 만드는 방법을 아는 것이 중요해요.

Unit 2

셀 수 있는 명사

1. 명사란 무엇인가?

명사는 사람이나 동물, 사물, 장소, 나라 등 이름을 가지고 있는 모든 것들을 나타내는 말이다.
또한 명사는 셀 수 있는 명사와 셀 수 없는 명사가 있다.

■ 종류

   (1) 셀 수 있는 명사

     → dog 개, cup 컵, book 책, student 학생, family 가족, team 팀

   (2) 셀 수 없는 명사

     → Korea 한국, Sunday 일요일, water 물, gold 금, love 사랑, air 공기

2. 셀 수 있는 명사

셀 수 있는 명사는 보통 일정한 형태가 있어서 하나, 둘, 셋, … 하고 개수를 셀 수 있다.

(1) 하나씩 구분할 수 있는 일정한 모양이 있는 명사(보통명사)

   ex. cat 고양이, teacher 선생님, bird 새, ball 공, boy 소년

(2) 사람이나 사물이 여럿 모여서 하나의 집합체를 이루는 명사(집합명사)

   ex. family 가족, class 학급, team 팀

3. 단수와 복수

명사의 개수가 하나이면 단수형으로, 둘 이상이면 복수형으로 나타낸다.

(1) 단수: 명사의 개수가 하나인 것을 말한다. 보통 명사 앞에 '하나의'라는 의미로 a나 an을 붙인다.

　　ex. a house 집, a girl 소녀, a chair 의자

(2) 복수: 명사의 개수가 둘 이상인 것을 말한다. 명사의 끝에 -s나 -es를 붙여서 복수형을 나타낸다.

　　ex. houses 집들, girls 소녀들, chairs 의자들

> **Pop Quiz** ┃ **1.** 다음 중 셀 수 있는 명사에 동그라미 하세요.
> 　　　　　　　→ book　water　family　time　student　team

4. 복수형 만드는법

우리말에서는 명사 뒤에 '~들'을 붙여 복수를 나타내지만, 영어에서는 명사 뒤에 -s나 -es를 붙여서 복수를 나타낸다.

(1) 규칙 변화

만드는 법		예
대부분의 명사	-s를 붙인다.	dog 개 → dogs 개들 house 집 → houses 집들 egg 계란 → eggs 계란들
-o, -s, -sh, -ch, -x로 끝나는 명사	-es를 붙인다.	potato 감자 → potatoes 감자들 bus 버스 → buses 버스들 dish 접시 → dishes 접시들 bench 벤치 → benches 벤치들 box 상자 → boxes 상자들
	예외	piano 피아노 → pianos 피아노들 cello 첼로 → cellos 첼로들 radio 라디오 → radios 라디오들

자음+y로 끝나는 명사	-y를 i로 바꾸고 -es를 붙인다.	family 가족 → families 가족들 city 도시 → cities 도시들 baby 아기 → babies 아기들 lady 숙녀 → ladies 숙녀들 candy 사탕 → candies 사탕들
모음+y로 끝나는 명사	-s를 붙인다.	boy 소년 → boys 소년들 toy 장난감 → toys 장난감들
-f(e)로 끝나는 명사	-f(e)를 v로 바꾸고 -es를 붙인다.	leaf 나뭇잎 → leaves 나뭇잎들 wolf 늑대 → wolves 늑대들 knife 칼 → knives 칼들
	예외	roof 지붕 → roofs 지붕들 chief 추장 → chiefs 추장들

(2) 불규칙 변화

만드는 법	예
단수와 복수의 형태가 같은 명사	fish 물고기 → fish 물고기들, deer 사슴 → deer 사슴들, sheep 양 → sheep 양들, salmon 연어 → salmon 연어들
단수와 복수의 형태가 전혀 다른 명사	foot 발 → feet 발들, tooth 치아 → teeth 치아들, woman 여자 → women 여자들, goose 거위 → geese 거위들, child 어린이 → children 어린이들, ox 황소 → oxen 황소들, mouse 쥐 → mice 쥐들

Pop Quiz **2.** 다음 중 명사의 복수형에 동그라미 하세요.
❶ dish (dishs, dishes) ❷ piano (pianos, pianoes)

다음 중 셀 수 있는 명사에 동그라미 하세요.

1	notebook	tree	water
2	love	apple	cat
3	Korea	student	chair
4	house	Sunday	dog
5	computer	potato	milk
6	tiger	doctor	family
7	woman	box	dish
8	coffee	window	bed
9	mouse	time	class
10	team	knife	boat
11	album	Canada	church
12	teacher	bike	bird
13	fish	picture	juice
14	baby	roof	bus
15	bench	Monday	goose
16	ball	flower	peace

love 사랑
Sunday 일요일
doctor 의사
church 교회
picture 그림, 사진
peace 평화

 Check Up 2

다음 괄호 안에서 명사의 복수형에 동그라미 하세요.

map 지도
foot 발
leaf 나뭇잎
watch 손목시계

1 dog   (dogs, doges)

2 map   (maps, mapes)

3 potato   (potatos, potatoes)

4 family   (familys, families)

5 man   (manes, men)

6 foot   (foots, feet)

7 watch   (watchs, watches)

8 leaf   (leafs, leaves)

9 piano   (pianos, pianoes)

10 lion   (lions, liones)

11 mouse   (mouses, mice)

12 sister   (sisters, sisteres)

13 bench   (benchs, benches)

14 baby   (babys, babies)

15 child   (childs, children)

16 book   (books, bookes)

다음 괄호 안에서 명사의 복수형에 동그라미 하세요.

1 city   (citys, cities)

2 dish   (dishs, dishes)

3 computer   (computers, computeres)

4 box   (boxs, boxes)

5 ox   (oxes, oxen)

6 tomato   (tomatos, tomatoes)

7 radio   (radios, radioes)

8 wolf   (wolf, wolves)

9 bag   (bags, bages)

10 dress   (dresses, dress)

11 sheep   (sheeps, sheep)

12 monkey   (monkeys, monkies)

13 mother   (mothers, motheres)

14 candy   (candys, candies)

15 roof   (roofs, rooves)

16 fish   (fishs, fish)

city 도시
ox 황소
radio 라디오
dress 드레스
sheep 양
roof 지붕

Step 1　**Check Up 4**

다음 괄호 안에서 명사의 복수형에 동그라미 하세요.

1	ruler	(rulers, ruleres)
2	mailman	(mailmans, mailmen)
3	butterfly	(butterflys, butterflies)
4	toy	(toys, toies)
5	class	(class, classes)
6	kid	(kids, kides)
7	desk	(desks, deskes)
8	country	(countrys, countries)
9	wife	(wifes, wives)
10	spoon	(spoons, spoones)
11	team	(teams, teames)
12	tray	(trays, traies)
13	peach	(peachs, peaches)
14	tooth	(toothes, teeth)
15	carrot	(carrots, carrotes)
16	day	(days, dayes)

ruler 자
mailman 우편배달부
kid 어린이
country 나라
tray 쟁반
peach 복숭아
carrot 당근

다음 중 알맞은 명사의 복수형을 고르고 빈칸에 쓰세요.

fly 파리
rose 장미
gentleman 신사
salmon 연어
hospital 병원

1	fly	☐ flies	☐ flie	_____
2	lemon	☐ lemons	☐ lemones	_____
3	party	☐ partys	☐ parties	_____
4	knife	☐ knifes	☐ knives	_____
5	foot	☐ foot	☐ feet	_____
6	fish	☐ fish	☐ fishs	_____
7	bench	☐ benches	☐ benchs	_____
8	mailman	☐ mailmans	☐ mailmen	_____
9	rose	☐ roses	☐ rosess	_____
10	dress	☐ dresses	☐ dress	_____
11	gentleman	☐ gentleman	☐ gentlemen	_____
12	salmon	☐ salmen	☐ salmon	_____
13	family	☐ families	☐ familis	_____
14	boy	☐ boys	☐ boies	_____
15	hospital	☐ hospitals	☐ hospitales	_____
16	leaf	☐ leafs	☐ leaves	_____

다음 주어진 명사들을 복수형을 만드는 규칙에 따라 고쳐 쓰세요.

> dish dog boy egg bus house toy potato day
> roof city candy knife family bench wolf box
> piano radio lady cello leaf chief baby

city 도시
bench 벤치
wolf 늑대
cello 첼로
radio 라디오

1 일반적으로 '-s'만 붙이는 명사

_____

2 '자음+y'로 끝나는 명사: y를 빼고+-ies

_____

3 '모음+y'로 끝나는 명사: +-s

_____

4 '-o, -s, -sh, -ch, -x'로 끝나는 명사: +es

_____

5 '-o'로 끝나는 명사 중 예외 단어: +s

_____

6 '-f(e)'로 끝나는 명사: f(e)를 빼고 +ves

_____

7 '-f(e)'로 끝나는 명사 중 예외 단어: +s

_____

Step 2 | Build Up 1

다음 명사의 복수형을 쓰세요.

knife 칼
candy 사탕
kite 연
dragonfly 잠자리

1 box _____

2 book _____

3 ox _____

4 knife _____

5 foot _____

6 candy _____

7 banana _____

8 class _____

9 bus _____

10 tomato _____

11 kite _____

12 fish _____

13 mailman _____

14 dragonfly _____

15 piano _____

16 wife _____

다음 명사의 복수형을 쓰세요.

ax 도끼
lemon 레몬
thief 도둑
vase 꽃병
fox 여우

1	roof	_____
2	watch	_____
3	ax	_____
4	robot	_____
5	woman	_____
6	lemon	_____
7	key	_____
8	thief	_____
9	ball	_____
10	child	_____
11	mouse	_____
12	fox	_____
13	deer	_____
14	vase	_____
15	cello	_____
16	dress	_____

다음 명사의 단수형을 쓰세요.

1 dishes _____

2 children _____

3 comedies _____

4 flags _____

5 geese _____

6 roofs _____

7 mice _____

8 deer _____

9 tomatoes _____

10 butterflies _____

11 classrooms _____

12 oxen _____

13 pianos _____

14 countries _____

15 watches _____

16 wolves _____

comedy 코미디, 희극

flag 깃발

goose 거위

classroom 교실

country 나라

 Jump Up 1

다음 빈칸에 알맞은 말을 쓰세요.

1 셀 수 있는 명사에는 보통명사와 _____가 있는데, _____는 하나씩 구분할 수 있는 일정한 모양이 있는 명사이고 _____는 사람이나 사물이 여럿 모여서 하나의 _____를 이루는 명사이다.

2 복수형 만드는 규칙

만드는 법		예
대부분의 명사	-s를 붙인다.	dog → _____ house → _____
-o, -s, -sh, -ch, -x로 끝나는 명사	-_____를 붙인다.	potato → potatoes bus → _____ dish → dishes bench → _____ box → _____
	예외	piano → _____
자음+y로 끝나는 명사	-y를 i로 바꾸고 -_____를 붙인다.	family → _____ baby → babies
모음+y로 끝나는 명사	-s를 붙인다.	boy → _____ toy → _____
-f(e)로 끝나는 명사	-f(e)를 _____로 바꾸고 -es를 붙인다.	leaf → leaves knife → _____
	예외	roof → _____
불규칙 변화	같거나 전혀 다른 명사	deer → _____ tooth → _____

다음 명사의 복수형을 쓰세요.

		nurse 간호사
1	nurse	_____
2	lady	_____
3	ruler	_____
4	salmon	_____
5	hat	_____
6	peach	_____
7	chair	_____
8	fisherman	_____
9	student	_____
10	tray	_____
11	radio	_____
12	glass	_____
13	church	_____
14	monkey	_____
15	party	_____
16	match	_____

nurse 간호사
hat 모자
fisherman 어부
glass 유리컵
church 교회
match 성냥
tray 쟁반

다음 명사의 복수형을 바르게 고쳐 쓰세요.

	단수형	복수형	
1	goose	gooses	_____
2	ox	oxes	_____
3	city	citys	_____
4	toothbrush	teethbrush	_____
5	toy	toies	_____
6	deer	deers	_____
7	watch	watchs	_____
8	piano	pianoes	_____
9	child	childes	_____
10	dragonfly	dragonflys	_____
11	mouse	mouses	_____
12	potato	potatos	_____
13	policeman	policemans	_____
14	museum	museumes	_____
15	family	familys	_____
16	wolf	wolfes	_____

toothbrush 칫솔
toy 장난감
policeman 경찰
museum 박물관

다음 빈칸에 명사의 복수형을 넣어 문장을 완성하세요.

1 She doesn't like _____. (mouse)

2 There are many _____ on the road. (bus)

3 Some _____ are playing soccer. (child)

4 He buys a lot of _____. (apple)

5 The kid is brushing the _____. (tooth)

6 She has three _____. (baby)

7 There are some _____. (dish)

8 Jamie has many _____. (flower)

9 The _____ are smart. (fox)

10 There are five _____ in the farm. (deer)

11 They have a lot of _____. (friend)

12 The _____ are falling. (leaf)

13 Kate has a lot of _____. (dress)

14 All the _____ are blue. (roof)

15 Those are tall _____. (building)

16 Two _____ are on the bench. (woman)

road 길
soccer 축구
buy 사다
flower 꽃
smart 영리한
farm 농장
building 빌딩

1 다음 중 셀 수 있는 명사가 <u>아닌</u> 것을 고르세요.

① house   ② book   ③ gas   ④ dog

2 다음 중 셀 수 있는 명사를 고르세요.

① Korea   ② apple
③ water   ④ love

[3~4] 다음 중 단수형과 복수형이 <u>잘못</u> 연결된 것을 고르세요.

3 ① bus – buses
② student – students
③ watch – watches
④ toy – toies

4 ① leaf – leafs
② deer – deer
③ child – children
④ ox – oxen

5 다음 중 명사의 복수형이 <u>아닌</u> 것을 고르세요.

① fish   ② axes   ③ tooth   ④ mice

[6~8] 다음 중 명사의 복수형 만드는 방법이 <u>다른</u> 것을 고르세요.

6 ① day   ② candy
③ family   ④ comedy

7 ① piano   ② potato
③ radio   ④ cello

8 ① tomato   ② bench
③ dish   ④ woman

[9~10] 다음 중 명사의 단수형을 복수형으로 바르게 고친 것을 고르세요.

9 ① salmon → salmones
② tray → traies
③ chief → chiefs
④ man → mans

10 ① box → boxen
② roof → rooves
③ party → parties
④ sheep → sheeps

11 다음 중 밑줄 친 부분을 바르게 고친 것을 고르세요.

He has eight <u>goose</u>.

① goose   ② gooses
③ geese   ④ goosen

12 다음 중 밑줄 친 부분에 들어갈 수 <u>없는</u> 것을 고르세요.

They have a _____.

① baby   ② children
③ ruler   ④ watch

[13~14] 다음 빈칸에 들어갈 말이 순서대로 짝 지어진 것을 고르세요.

13

We have one _____ and two _____.

① lemon – peaches
② lemons – peach
③ lemon – peach
④ lemons – peaches

14

I need one _____ and five _____.

① knife – dishs
② knife – dishes
③ knifes – dish
④ knives – dishes

15 다음 중 빈칸에 들어갈 말을 고르세요.

Do you have two _____?

① tray
② carrot
③ vase
④ flowers

16 다음 빈칸에 들어갈 알맞은 말을 쓰세요.
The kid has three _____. (사탕들)

[17~19] 다음 중 바르지 않은 문장을 고르세요.

17
① There are three deer.
② Two cats are in the room.
③ We need ten chaires.
④ I have six brushes.

18
① They have three children.
② I buy five apples.
③ All the roofs are red.
④ We have two knifes.

19
① There are ten bench in the park.
② There are two doors in my office.
③ There are eight fish in the pond.
④ There is a man in the bank.

[20~22] 다음 빈칸에 명사의 복수형을 넣어 문장을 완성하세요.

20 She doesn't like _____. (wolf)

21 The child is brushing the _____. (tooth)

22 Mom has a lot of _____. (dress)

[23~25] 다음 밑줄 친 부분을 바르게 고쳐 문장을 다시 쓰세요.

23 I see two policemans.
→ _____.

24 The dogs have four foot.
→ _____.

25 Five dish are on the table.
→ _____.

서술형 평가

A Jack이 길을 잃어버렸는데, 스핑크스가 낸 퀴즈를 풀면 돌아갈 수 있습니다. 스핑크스의 퀴즈를 풀어 보세요.

family, knife
city, lady
wolf, leaf

rose, chair
student, foot
deer, child

1 주어진 명사들을 복수형 만드는 규칙에 따라 고쳐 쓰세요.

-s만 붙이는 명사	y를 빼고 +-ies를 붙이는 명사	f(e)를 빼고 +ves를 붙이는 명사

2 1에서 분류되지 않은 3개의 단어를 찾아 복수형을 쓰고, 공통점도 쓰세요.

_____ _____ _____ 공통점: _____

B 다음 그림을 보고, 빈칸에 알맞은 말을 쓰세요.

1 There are two _____ on the road. (bus)

2 There are five _____ on the field. (sheep)

3 The baby has only five _____. (tooth)

셀 수 없는 명사

셀 수 없는 명사를 이해할 수 있다.

셀 수 없는 명사의 많고 적음을 나타내는 방법을 알 수 있다.

셀 수 없는 명사는 일정한 형태가 없는 물질이나 재료, 또는 눈에 보이지 않는 추상적인 것들의 이름이며, 일정한 형태가 없고 눈에 보이지 않아 개수를 셀 수 가 없어요. 이렇 기 때문에 셀 수 없는 명사는 명사 자체만으로는 복수형을 만들 수 없으며 용기나 단위 등을 이용하여 수량을 나타낼 수 있어요.

Unit 3

셀 수 없는 명사

1. 셀 수 없는 명사의 특징

셀 수 없는 명사는 일정한 형태가 없는 물질이나 재료, 또는 눈에 보이지 않는 추상적인 것들의 이름이다. 일정한 형태가 없고 눈에 보이지 않아 개수를 셀 수가 없다.

(1) '하나'를 나타내는 a, an과 함께 쓰지 않는다. a milk (×)

(2) 명사의 복수형을 만들 수가 없다. waters (×)

(3) 단위를 나타내는 말과 함께 복수형을 만들 수 있다. two cups of water

2. 셀 수 없는 명사

셀 수 없는 명사에는 고유명사, 물질명사, 추상명사가 있다.

(1) 고유명사: 이름이나 장소 등과 같이 세상에 오직 하나밖에 없는 명사

사람 이름	Kate, Jamie, Jay, Mr. Brown, Eric
도시, 국가의 이름	Seoul 서울, London 런던, China 중국, Europe 유럽
명절, 축제의 이름	New Year's Day 새해 첫날, Christmas 크리스마스
요일, 달의 이름	Sunday 일요일, Monday 월요일, January 1월, April 4월

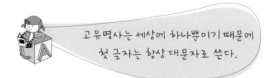

고유명사는 세상에 하나뿐이기 때문에
첫 글자는 항상 대문자로 쓴다.

(2) 물질명사: 일정한 모양과 크기가 없는 물질이나 재료로 이루어진 명사

기체	air 공기, gas 가스
액체	oil 기름, shampoo 샴푸, juice 주스, milk 우유, water 물, coffee 커피, tea 차, soup 수프, honey 꿀, ink 잉크
고체	furniture 가구, gold 금, silver 은, soap 비누, bread 빵, cheese 치즈, pizza 피자, butter 버터, rice 쌀, sugar 설탕, salt 소금, paper 후추, sand 모래, stone 석재, wood 목재, steel 철, paper 종이, plastic 플라스틱
자연 현상	rain 비, snow 눈, sunshine 햇빛, wind 바람, cloud 구름

Pop Quiz

1. 다음 중 고유명사에는 ○표, 물질명사에는 △표 하세요.

→ gold rain Seoul milk Monday salt ink

(3) 추상명사: 뚜렷한 모양 없이 추상적인 개념을 나타내는 명사

과목	math 수학, music 음악, art 미술, history 역사, science 과학
운동	soccer 축구, baseball 야구, tennis 테니스, golf 골프
생각이나 감정	love 사랑, hope 희망, friendship 우정, advice 충고
기타	energy 에너지, time 시간, help 도움, work 일, e-mail 이메일, peace 평화, war 전쟁, information 정보

3. 셀 수 없는 명사의 수량 표현

셀수 없는 명사는 개수를 나타낼 수 없기 때문에 용기나 단위 등을 이용하여 수량을 나타낼 수 있다. 이 때 숫자 뒤의 용기나 단위를 나타내는 명사를 복수형으로 쓰고 셀 수 없는 명사는 단수형으로 쓴다.

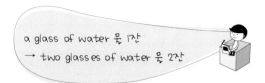

a glass of water 물 1잔
→ two glasses of water 물 2잔

단위	뜻	셀 수 없는 명사
a cup of	~ 1컵(잔)	coffee 커피, tea 차, water 물
a glass of	~ 1잔	juice 주스, water 물, milk 우유
a bottle of	~ 1병	juice 주스, milk 우유, water 물, ink 잉크, shampoo 샴푸
a slice (piece) of	~ 1조각	bread 빵, cake 케이크, cheese 치즈, pizza 피자, paper 종이
a bowl of	~ 1그릇	rice 쌀, soup 수프, salad 샐러드
a loaf of	~ 1 덩어리	bread 빵, cheese 치즈, butter 버터, meat 고기
a sheet of	~ 1장	paper 종이
a bag of	~ 1봉지	rice 쌀, sugar 설탕, salt 소금
a kilo of	~ 1킬로	salt 소금, sugar 설탕, flour 밀가루
a liter of	~ 1리터	milk 우유, water 물, juice 주스
a spoonful of	~ 1 숟가락	salt 소금, sugar 설탕, pepper 후추, rice 쌀, oil 기름
a bar of	~ 1 개	chocolate 초콜릿, soap 비누
a pound of	~ 1파운드	sugar 설탕, salt 소금, flour 밀가루
a bunch of	~ 1송이(다발)	grapes 포도, bananas 바나나, roses 장미, flowers 꽃

Pop Quiz **2. 다음 괄호 안에서 알맞은 것을 고르세요.**

❶ two (cup, cups) of tea   ❷ a (bottle, bar) of milk

다음 중 셀 수 없는 명사에 동그라미 하세요.

1	brother	air	tiger
2	bread	boy	rice
3	teacher	April	war
4	tea	table	cat
5	house	paper	cheese
6	bike	time	music
7	butter	gas	clock
8	dish	gold	bed
9	sand	bird	class
10	man	train	Jane
11	Canada	tree	sugar
12	store	love	Seoul
13	salt	student	family
14	juice	milk	math
15	door	Monday	foot
16	ball	oil	wind

air 공기
rice 쌀
bike 자전거
clock 시계
train 기차
oil 기름
wind 바람

다음 셀 수 없는 명사의 종류로 알맞은 것을 고르세요.

plastic 플라스틱
pepper 후추
advice 충고
help 도움
furniture 가구
paint 페인트

1	rain	(고유명사, 물질명사, 추상명사)
2	New York	(고유명사, 물질명사, 추상명사)
3	plastic	(고유명사, 물질명사, 추상명사)
4	pepper	(고유명사, 물질명사, 추상명사)
5	advice	(고유명사, 물질명사, 추상명사)
6	Friday	(고유명사, 물질명사, 추상명사)
7	help	(고유명사, 물질명사, 추상명사)
8	e-mail	(고유명사, 물질명사, 추상명사)
9	gas	(고유명사, 물질명사, 추상명사)
10	furniture	(고유명사, 물질명사, 추상명사)
11	China	(고유명사, 물질명사, 추상명사)
12	April	(고유명사, 물질명사, 추상명사)
13	baseball	(고유명사, 물질명사, 추상명사)
14	paint	(고유명사, 물질명사, 추상명사)
15	Christmas	(고유명사, 물질명사, 추상명사)
16	butter	(고유명사, 물질명사, 추상명사)

다음 상자 안의 명사들을 분류에 맞게 골라 쓰세요.

tennis science sugar Tuesday March July energy
milk bread Korea hope soccer snow honey
London Seoul sand peace silver soup

July 7월
soup 수프
honey 꿀
science 과학
soccer 축구
energy 에너지

| 고유명사

_____ _____ _____

_____ _____ _____

2 물질명사

_____ _____ _____

_____ _____ _____

_____ _____

3 추상명사

_____ _____ _____

_____ _____ _____

다음 우리말과 같도록 알맞은 것을 골라 동그라미 하세요.

meat 고기
paper 종이
salt 소금
soap 비누
flour 밀가루

1 차 1잔   a (cup, bottle) of tea

2 물 1잔   a (loaf, glass) of water

3 우유 1병   a (bar, bottle) of milk

4 케이크 1조각   a (piece, pound) of cake

5 밥 1그릇   a (bowl, bag) of rice

6 고기 1 덩어리   a (cup, loaf) of meat

7 종이 1장   a (liter, sheet) of paper

8 포도 1송이   a (bunch, pound) of grapes

9 소금 1파운드   a (bowl, pound) of salt

10 비누 1개   a (bar, glass) of soap

11 치즈 1조각   a (slice, loaf) of cheese

12 기름 1 숟가락   a (sheet, spoonful) of oil

13 밀가루 1킬로   a (kilo, liter) of flour

14 설탕 1봉지   a (bunch, bag) of sugar

15 주스 1잔   a (bottle, glass) of juice

16 물 1리터   a (liter, piece) of water

다음 우리말과 같도록 알맞은 것을 골라 동그라미 하세요.

1	케이크 4조각	four (slices, slice) of cake
2	초콜릿 2개	two (bar, bars) of chocolate
3	밀가루 2파운드	two pounds of (flour, flours)
4	설탕 5킬로	five (kilo, kilos) of sugar
5	소금 6 숟가락	six spoonfuls of (salt, salts)
6	우유 2잔	two glasses of (milk, milks)
7	빵 2조각	two (pieces, loaves) of bread
8	커피 3잔	three (cups, bars) of coffee
9	샐러드 2그릇	two (bowl, bowls) of salad
10	잉크 4병	four bottles of (ink, inks)
11	주스 2리터	two (liters, kilos) of juice
12	포도 2송이	two bunches of (grape, grapes)
13	치즈 3조각	three (slice, slices) of cheese
14	쌀 2봉지	two (cups, bags) of rice
15	종이 5장	five sheets of (paper, papers)
16	버터 2 덩어리	two (loaf, loaves) of butter

chocolate 초콜릿
bread 빵
salad 샐러드
ink 잉크
butter 버터

Step 1

Check Up 6

다음 우리말과 같도록 알맞은 것을 골라 동그라미 하세요

shampoo 샴푸
pizza 피자
banana 바나나

1 빵 1 덩어리   a (loaf, loaves) of bread

2 샴푸 6통   six bottles of (shampoo, shampoos)

3 종이 3장   three (sheets, bunches) of paper

4 피자 2조각   two (piece, pieces) of pizza

5 바나나 1다발   a bunch of (banana, bananas)

6 비누 6개   six (bar, bars) of (soap, soaps)

7 우유 4병   four (liters, bottles) of milk

8 쌀 2봉지   two (bag, bags) of (rice, rices)

9 치즈 1조각   a (piece, pieces) of cheese

10 커피 3잔   three (cup, cups) of (coffee, coffees)

11 설탕 2 숟가락   two (spoonful, spoonfuls) of sugar

12 주스 1리터   a (liter, liters) of (juice, juices)

13 수프 3그릇   three (bowl, bowls) of soup

14 소금 2파운드   two pounds of (salt, salts)

15 후추 1킬로   a (kilo, kilos) of pepper

16 포도 4송이   four bunches of (grape, grapes)

Build Up 1

다음 문장의 밑줄 친 부분을 바르게 고쳐 쓰세요.

1	I like <u>rains</u>.	→	_____
2	We drink <u>milks</u>.	→	_____
3	I need <u>times</u>.	→	_____
4	Give me <u>waters</u>.	→	_____
5	They live in <u>seoul</u>.	→	_____
6	We want <u>loves</u>.	→	_____
7	I like <u>sunday</u>.	→	_____
8	I eat <u>breads</u>.	→	_____
9	You like <u>cheeses</u>.	→	_____
10	Give me <u>sugars</u>.	→	_____
11	They like <u>christmas</u>.	→	_____
12	I know <u>jamie</u>.	→	_____
13	We need <u>sunshines</u>.	→	_____
14	I drink <u>juices</u>.	→	_____
15	I visit Mr. <u>white</u>.	→	_____
16	They need <u>hopes</u>.	→	_____

drink 마시다
live 살다
know 알다
visit 방문하다
sunshine 햇빛
hope 희망

셀 수 없는 명사 · **63**

다음 문장의 빈칸에 알맞은 것을 고르고, 빈칸에 쓰세요.

ink 잉크
want 원하다
oil 기름
flour 밀가루

1 Give me a _____ of water. (☐ glass ☐ loaf)

2 I have two _____ of bread. (☐ piece ☐ pieces)

3 We need a _____ of sugar. (☐ bunch ☐ pound)

4 They buy three _____ of ink. (☐ bottles ☐ bars)

5 I want four _____ of paper. (☐ liters ☐ sheets)

6 You drink a _____ of tea. (☐ bowl ☐ cup)

7 I need two _____ of oil. (☐ spoonfuls ☐ bowls)

8 We want two _____ of flour. (☐ liters ☐ kilos)

9 I buy five _____ of grapes. (☐ bunches ☐ bars)

10 Give me a _____ of salad. (☐ slice ☐ bowl)

11 They drink two _____ of juice. (☐ liter ☐ liters)

12 I have four _____ of soap. (☐ bars ☐ glasses)

13 They eat six _____ of pizza. (☐ bags ☐ pieces)

14 I need a _____ of meat. (☐ cup ☐ loaf)

15 You have two _____ of cheese. (☐ slices ☐ bars)

16 We buy two _____ of rice. (☐ bag ☐ bags)

다음 우리말과 같도록 빈칸에 영어로 쓰세요.

soap 비누
paper 종이
butter 버터

1 비누 4개 _____

2 우유 2잔 _____

3 빵 5 덩어리 _____

4 물 2병 _____

5 쌀 2봉지 _____

6 포도 3송이 _____

7 종이 9장 _____

8 주스 3리터 _____

9 밀가루 6파운드 _____

10 커피 7잔 _____

11 수프 4그릇 _____

12 케이크 3조각 _____

13 기름 2 숟가락 _____

14 설탕 4킬로 _____

15 버터 2 덩어리 _____

16 피자 8조각 _____

다음 빈칸에 알맞은 말을 쓰세요.

Ⅰ 셀 수 없는 명사는 일정한 형태가 없는 물질이나 재료, 또는 눈에 보이지 않는 추상적인 것들의 _____이
다. 셀 수 없는 명사에는 _____, _____, _____가 있다.

(1) '하나'를 나타내는 _____, _____과 함께 쓰지 않는다. a milk (×)

(2) 명사의 _____을 만들 수가 없다. waters (×)

(3) 단위를 나타내는 말과 함께 _____을 만들 수 있다. two cups of tea

2 셀 수 없는 명사의 수량 표현

단위	뜻	단위를 이용한 수량 표현	
a cup of	~ 1컵(잔)	차 2잔	→ two cups of tea
a glass of	~ 1잔	물 1잔	→ _____
a bottle of	~ 1병	_____	→ three bottles of ink
a slice(piece) of	~ 1조각	케이크 1조각	→ _____
a bowl of	~ 1그릇	수프 4그릇	→ _____
a loaf of	~ 1 덩어리	_____	→ two loaves of butter
a sheet of	~ 1장	_____	→ six sheets of paper
a bag of	~ 1봉지	쌀 5봉지	→ _____
a kilo of	~ 1킬로	_____	→ a kilo of flour
a liter of	~ 1리터	우유 2리터	→ _____
a spoonful of	~ 1 숟가락	기름 1 숟가락	→ _____
a bar of	~ 1개	_____	→ four bars of soap
a pound of	~ 1파운드	설탕 2파운드	→ _____
a bunch of	~ 1송이(다발)	포도 1송이	→ _____

다음에서 밑줄 친 부분을 바르게 고쳐 쓰세요.

1	three cups of <u>coffees</u>	_____
2	five <u>loaf</u> of butter	_____
3	seven bunches of <u>grape</u>	_____
4	a <u>bottles</u> of shampoo	_____
5	ten <u>pieces</u> of soap	_____
6	two <u>pound</u> of flour	_____
7	four <u>pieces</u> of bananas	_____
8	a <u>sheets</u> of paper	_____
9	three loaves of <u>meats</u>	_____
10	ten <u>bar</u> of chocolate	_____
11	two <u>spoonful</u> of pepper	_____
12	four liters of <u>waters</u>	_____
13	nine bowls of <u>salads</u>	_____
14	three <u>slices</u> of soup	_____
15	eight kilos of <u>sugars</u>	_____
16	a <u>loaves</u> of bread	_____

shampoo 샴푸
soap 비누
meat 고기
pepper 후추

다음 문장에서 밑줄 친 부분의 우리말 뜻을 빈칸에 쓰세요.

butter 버터
salad 샐러드
salt 소금
orange juice 오렌지 주스
chocolate 초콜릿

1   Give me two sheets of paper.   _____

2   I have a pound of sugar.   _____

3   We drink two glasses of water.   _____

4   I buy two loaves of butter.   _____

5   You need five bottles of juice.   _____

6   Give me three pieces of cake.   _____

7   I eat four bowls of salad.   _____

8   They want two spoonfuls of salt.   _____

9   I need a kilo of sugar.   _____

10 There are five pieces of cheese.   _____

11 I want three cups of coffee.   _____

12 You drink a glass of orange juice.   _____

13 They eat eight pieces of pizza.   _____

14 Give me two liters of milk.   _____

15 We need six bars of chocolate.   _____

16 I have two bunches of bananas.   _____

다음 우리말과 같도록 빈칸에 알맞은 말을 쓰세요.

1 I eat _____. (빵 2조각)

2 We buy _____. (밀가루 3킬로)

3 They eat _____. (피자 1조각)

4 Give me _____. (커피 5잔)

5 You have _____. (소금 2봉지)

6 I buy _____. (주스 4병)

7 They drink _____. (우유 6잔)

8 I need _____. (고기 2 덩어리)

9 I want _____. (종이 1장)

10 Give me _____. (잉크 3병)

11 We eat _____. (초콜릿 4개)

12 I need _____. (설탕 1 숟가락)

13 We have _____. (포도 2송이)

14 Give me _____. (밥 5그릇)

15 I have _____. (물 1리터)

16 They eat _____. (수프 3그릇)

1 다음 중 셀 수 없는 명사를 고르세요.

① computer　　② information

③ television　　④ window

2 다음 중 셀 수 없는 명사가 <u>아닌</u> 것을 고르세요.

① Sunday　　② science

③ coffee　　④ family

3 다음 중 물질명사를 고르세요.

① advice　　② grapes

③ pepper　　④ New York

4 다음 중 추상명사를 고르세요.

① energy　　② juice

③ Christmas　　④ flower

5 다음 중 고유명사가 <u>아닌</u> 것을 고르세요.

① Friday　　② Korea

③ sunshine　　④ Jane

6 다음 중 바르지 <u>않은</u> 것을 고르세요.

① a cup of tea

② two loaves of butters

③ a bunch of bananas

④ four slices of cheese

[7~8] 다음 문장의 빈칸에 알맞은 말을 고르세요.

7

> We drink a _____ of milk.

① glass　　② sheet

③ bag　　④ piece

8

> I buy a _____ of soap.

① bottle　　② cup

③ bar　　④ liter

[9~10] 다음 중 밑줄 친 부분이 올바른 것을 고르세요.

9 ① Give me <u>waters</u>.

② They live in <u>seoul</u>.

③ I eat <u>breads</u>.

④ I need <u>time</u>.

10 ① We want <u>loves</u>.

② I drink <u>juice</u>.

③ You like <u>cheeses</u>.

④ I know <u>James</u>.

[11~12] 다음 우리말과 같도록 괄호 안에서 알맞은 것을 고르세요.

11 우리는 샐러드 3그릇을 먹는다.

We eat three (bowl, bowls) of (salad, salads).

12 나는 설탕 2킬로가 필요하다.
I need two (liters, kilos) of
(sugar, sugars).

[13~14] 다음 빈칸에 들어갈 말이 순서대로 짝
지어진 것을 고르세요.

13
> I buy two _____ of rice and a
> _____ of meat.

① bag – loaf   ② bags – loaves
③ bags – loaf   ④ bag – loaves

14
> They eat four _____ of cake
> and a _____ of juice.

① pieces – kilo   ② pieces – liter
③ pound – liter   ④ pound – glass

15 다음 중 빈칸에 들어갈 말을 고르세요.

> I want a glass of _____.

① paper   ② chocolate
③ salt   ④ water

16 다음 문장의 빈칸에 알맞은 말을 쓰세요.
You eat a _____ of grapes.

[17~19] 다음 중 바르지 않은 문장을 고르세요.

17 ① We buy two kilos of flour.
② Give me a cup of coffee.

③ I buy four bottles of juice.
④ I need two loaf of meats.

18 ① Give me five bottles of milk.
② I need two spoonful of salt.
③ Give me five bowls of rice.
④ You eat three bowls of soup.

19 ① I eat three pieces of breads.
② You have two bags of salt.
③ They drink six glasses of water.
④ I want a sheet of paper.

[20~22] 다음 밑줄 친 부분을 바르게 고쳐 쓰
세요.

20 We eat four <u>bar</u> of chocolate.
→ _____

21 I want a <u>sheets</u> of paper.
→ _____

22 I have two liters of <u>milks</u>.
→ _____

[23~25] 다음 우리말과 같도록 빈칸에 알맞은
말을 쓰세요.

23 I eat _____. (치즈 3조각)

24 We buy _____. (밀가루 2파운드)

25 They have _____. (우유 4병)

서술형 평가

A 다음 그림을 보고, 물음에 답해 보세요.

bike   doctor   leaf   milk   water
sugar   love   peace
     paper
soccer   Korea   math
     Canada
Sunday   April

I 주어진 단어들 중 셀 수 없는 명사를 골라 써 보세요.

고유명사	물질명사	추상명사

2 1에서 분류되지 않은 3개의 단어를 찾아 쓰고, 공통점도 쓰세요.

_____ _____ _____   공통점: _____

B 다음 Sue의 식단표를 보고, 빈칸에 알맞은 말을 쓰세요.

	breakfast	lunch	dinner
Tuesday			

I Sue had a _____ of milk and two _____ of bread for breakfast.

2 Sue had a glass of _____, a _____ of salad and a _____ of pizza.

3 Sue had spaghetti for dinner. Then she had a _____ of green tea and a
_____ of grapes.

Unit 4

관사

관사의 역할과 종류 및 쓰임을 이해할 수 있다.

부정관사 a/an과 정관사 the를 구분하고 활용할 수 있다.

우리말과 달리 영어에서는 명사의 단수형에 관사가 붙어서 명사의 의미를 명확히 해 주는데, 명사 앞에 어떤 관사가 붙느냐에 따라서 그 의미가 달라져요. 가리키는 대상 (명사)이 정해져 있을 때는 the를 붙이고, 그 대상(명사)이 정해져 있지 않을 때는 a/an을 붙여요.

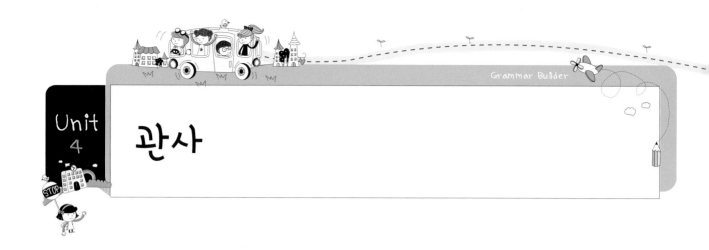

Unit 4 관사

1. 관사란 무엇인가요?

우리말과 달리 영어에서는 명사의 단수형 앞에 붙어서 명사의 의미를 명확히 해 주는데, 그 명사 앞에 붙는 말이 관사이다.

부정관사 a/an	정관사 the
• '하나의', '어떤'이라는 뜻이다. • 셀 수 있는 명사 앞에 붙는다. • 셀 수 있는 명사가 복수 명사이면 a/an을 붙이지 않으며 복수형을 쓴다. • 부정확한 대상 앞에 붙는다.	• '그'라는 뜻이다. • 셀 수 있는 명사와 셀 수 없는 명사 앞에 붙는다. • 복수 명사 앞에도 붙을 수 있다. • 정확한 대상 앞에 붙는다.

2. 부정관사 a/an

(1) 대부분의 명사 앞에는 a를 붙이지만, 첫소리가 모음 'a, e, i, o, u'로 소리 나는 명사 앞에는 an을 붙인다.

철자가 아닌 첫소리임에 유의한다.

a	book, chair, desk, flower, table, European, university ...
an	apple, egg, igloo, orange, umbrella, hour, Mp3 player ...

 주의 명사 앞에 명사를 꾸며주는 말이 있을 경우에는 명사의 첫소리가 아닌 그 꾸며주는 말의 첫소리에 따라서 a나 an을 붙인다.

a book 하나의 책, an easy book 하나의 쉬운 책

an umbrella 하나의 우산, a new umbrella 하나의 새 우산

(2) 부정관사 a/an의 쓰임

하나(=one)	I have a computer. 나는 컴퓨터 1대가 있다. There is a box on the sofa. 그 소파 위에 상자 1개가 있다.
(막연한) 어떤	A man is coming into the room. 어떤 남자가 방으로 들어오고 있다.
~마다(=per)	I eat three meals a day. 나는 하루에 3번 식사를 한다.

(3) a/an을 붙이지 않는 경우

❶ 고유명사, 복수명사 앞에: a Seoul (×), a Sunday (×), a cats (×)

❷ 셀 수 없는 명사 앞에: a milk (×), a paper (×), a peace (×)

❸ 소유격 앞에: a your baby (×), a my computer (×)

Pop Quiz I. 다음 괄호 안에서 알맞은 것을 고르세요.

❶ (a, an) university   ❷ (a, an) book   ❸ (a, an) orange

3. 정관사 the

가리키는 대상이 정확히 무엇인지 알 수 있는 경우에 사용하며 고유명사를 제외한 모든 명사 앞에 붙을 수 있다.

(1) 앞에 나온 명사가 다시 반복될 때

There is a baby. The baby is cute. 한 아기가 있다. 그 아기는 귀엽다.

(2) 서로 알고 있는 것을 가리킬 때

Open the window, please. 창문을 열어주세요.

(3) 세상에서 유일한 자연물 앞에: the earth, the moon, the sea, the sky

The earth goes around the sun. 지구는 태양 주위를 돈다.

(4) 강, 바다 이름이나 방향, 위치 앞에: the East Sea, the west, the left

People go to the south. 사람들이 남쪽으로 간다.

(5) 악기 이름 앞에: the piano, the violin, the guitar

I play the piano well. 나는 피아노를 잘 친다.

4. 관사를 쓰지 않는 경우

호칭으로 쓰일 때	Waiter, bring me a cup of coffee. 웨이터, 커피 한잔 부탁해요.
운동 이름 앞에	soccer, tennis, baseball, basketball, golf I play soccer. 나는 축구를 한다.
식사, 과목 앞에	breakfast, lunch, dinner, math, English, history, science I have lunch at twelve. 나는 12시에 점심을 먹는다. I like math very much. 나는 수학을 매우 좋아한다.
건물이 본래 목적으로 쓰일 때	go to school 학교(공부하러) 가다, go to church 교회(예배하러) 가다, go to bed 잠자리에(잠자기 위해) 들다
by＋교통수단	by＋bus(taxi, plane, car, bike) We go to the park by bus. 우리는 버스로 그 공원에 간다.

Pop Quiz   2. 다음 괄호 안에서 알맞은 것을 고르세요.

❶ play (×, the) golf   ❷ play (×, the) piano   ❸ by (×, the) bus

다음 괄호 안에서 알맞은 것을 골라 동그라미 하세요.

1 (a, an) actor

2 (a, an) box

3 (a, an) table

4 (a, an) university

5 (a, an) lion

6 (a, an) car

7 (a, an) apple

8 (a, an) woman

9 (a, an) scientist

10 (a, an) European

11 (a, an) rose

12 (a, an) orange

13 (a, an) octopus

14 (a, an) MP3 player

15 (a, an) computer

16 (a, an) uncle

17 (a, an) egg

18 (a, an) dog

19 (a, an) hour

20 (a, an) umbrella

21 (a, an) book

22 (a, an) igloo

23 (a, an) chair

24 (a, an) doll

25 (a, an) onion

26 (a, an) hat

27 (a, an) piano

28 (a, an) map

29 (a, an) honest boy

30 (a, an) ax

---

actor 배우

university 대학

scientist 과학자

octopus 문어

uncle 삼촌

onion 양파

hat 모자

map 지도

honest 정직한

다음 괄호 안에서 알맞은 것을 골라 동그라미 하세요.

1 (a, an, ×) children

2 (a, an, ×) ant

3 (a, an, ×) peace

4 (a, an, ×) team

5 (a, an, ×) milk

6 (a, an, ×) Korea

7 (a, an, ×) onion

8 (a, an, ×) family

9 (a, an, ×) my toy

10 (a, an, ×) music

11 (a, an, ×) teacher

12 (a, an, ×) water

13 (a, an, ×) eggs

14 (a, an, ×) cat

15 (a, an, ×) ox

16 (a, an, ×) wolf

17 (a, an, ×) Jane

18 (a, an, ×) alligator

19 (a, an, ×) apples

20 (a, an, ×) doll

21 (a, an, ×) bread

22 (a, an, ×) elephant

23 (a, an, ×) sugar

24 (a, an, ×) your box

25 (a, an, ×) ink

26 (a, an, ×) rain

27 (a, an, ×) Sunday

28 (a, an, ×) watch

29 (a, an, ×) singer

30 (a, an, ×) actors

ant 개미
peace 평화
toy 장난감
alligator 악어
elephant 코끼리
watch 손목시계
singer 가수

다음 명사 앞에 a나 an을 쓰고, 필요 없는 곳에는 ×를 쓰세요.

1 _____ door

2 _____ Seoul

3 _____ potatoes

4 _____ ant

5 _____ children

6 _____ university

7 _____ October

8 _____ hour

9 _____ oil

10 _____ salt

11 _____ igloo

12 _____ computer

13 _____ oranges

14 _____ actors

15 _____ bus

16 _____ umbrella

17 _____ my cat

18 _____ John

19 _____ birds

20 _____ MP3 CD

21 _____ men

22 _____ ugly boy

23 _____ bear

24 _____ cheese

25 _____ angel

26 _____ onion

27 _____ Japan

28 _____ window

29 _____ apple

30 _____ butter

potato 감자
igloo 이글루
butter 버터
ugly 못생긴
angel 천사
Japan 일본

Check Up 4

다음 명사 앞에 들어갈 말을 고르고, 쓰세요.(필요 없음은 ×를 하세요.)

| soccer 축구 |
| math 수학 |
| right 오른쪽 |
| lunch 점심 |
| moon 달 |
| basketball 농구 |

1 _____ soccer ☐ the ☐ 필요 없음

2 _____ sun ☐ the ☐ 필요 없음

3 _____ breakfast ☐ the ☐ 필요 없음

4 _____ piano ☐ the ☐ 필요 없음

5 _____ math ☐ the ☐ 필요 없음

6 _____ south ☐ the ☐ 필요 없음

7 _____ right ☐ the ☐ 필요 없음

8 _____ earth ☐ the ☐ 필요 없음

9 _____ lunch ☐ the ☐ 필요 없음

10 _____ baseball ☐ the ☐ 필요 없음

11 _____ cello ☐ the ☐ 필요 없음

12 _____ science ☐ the ☐ 필요 없음

13 _____ moon ☐ the ☐ 필요 없음

14 _____ basketball ☐ the ☐ 필요 없음

15 _____ west ☐ the ☐ 필요 없음

16 _____ dinner ☐ the ☐ 필요 없음

다음 괄호 안에서 알맞은 것을 골라 동그라미 하세요.

meal 식사

onion 양파

ax 도끼

church 교회

university 대학

long 긴

tail 꼬리

1 I have (a, an, ×) red umbrella.

2 I eat three meals (a, an, ×) day.

3 She has (a, an, ×) onion.

4 I like (a, an, ×) Tom very much.

5 It is (a, an, ×) yellow chair.

6 There are (a, an, ×) elephants.

7 This is (a, an, ×) my ax.

8 I go to church on (a, an, ×) Sunday.

9 There is (a, an, ×) university there.

10 We have three (a, an, ×) cats.

11 Give me (a, an, ×) water.

12 He is (a, an, ×) European.

13 I drink (a, an, ×) two glasses of milk.

14 (A, An, ×) Kate is (a, an, ×) honest girl.

15 I want (a, an, ×) egg and (a, an, ×) sugar.

16 (A, An, ×) alligator has (a, an, ×) long tail.

다음 괄호 안에서 알맞은 것을 골라 동그라미 하세요.

hot 뜨거운
moon 달
close 닫다
west 서쪽
speak 말하다
together 함께
guitar 기타

1 (The, ×) S(s)un is hot.

2 I like (the, ×) math.

3 (The, ×) S(s)ky is blue.

4 They go to (the, ×) bed at ten.

5 You like (the, ×) moon.

6 Close (the, ×) window.

7 We play (the, ×) violin well.

8 They have (the, ×) lunch.

9 Tom and Eric go to (the, ×) west.

10 Birds fly in (the, ×) sky.

11 I go to (the, ×) church every Sunday.

12 I can speak (the, ×) English.

13 We go to the park by (the, ×) bike.

14 They play (the, ×) soccer together.

15 Boys like (the, ×) science.

16 Alice can play (the, ×) guitar.

다음 문장의 빈칸에 the를 쓰고, 필요 없으면 ×표 하세요.

1 I meet _____ Julia on Monday.

2 You play _____ cello everyday.

3 _____ E(e)arth goes around _____ sun.

4 _____ B(b)reakfast is ready.

5 We play _____ soccer on Sundays.

6 There is a dog. _____ dog is mine.

7 They study _____ science.

8 We go to China by _____ plane.

9 Look at the clouds in _____ sky.

10 I have _____ dinner at seven o'clock.

11 There are many fish in _____ sea.

12 He goes to _____ bed at ten.

13 Open _____ window, _____ Jane.

14 They play _____ piano.

15 _____ W(w)aiter, bring me a cup of tea.

16 I have _____ lunch with my friends.

everyday 매일	
ready 준비가 된	
mine 나의 것	
China 중국	
cloud 구름	
sea 바다	
bring 가져오다	

다음 문장의 빈칸에 a(n)나 the를 쓰고, 필요 없으면 ×표 하세요.

1 This is _____ album.

2 We live on _____ earth.

3 There is _____ baby. _____ baby is cute.

4 They go to the bank by _____ car.

5 Give me _____ bag of sugar, please.

6 You have _____ orange.

7 _____ M(m)oon is round.

8 They go to _____ school.

9 I study math for _____ hour _____ day.

10 I have _____ breakfast at eight o'clock.

11 There are birds in _____ sky.

12 My father is _____ actor.

13 I play _____ guitar very much.

14 I play _____ baseball after school.

15 We see _____ European there.

16 Close _____ door, please.

album 앨범
live 살다
bank 은행
round 둥근
actor 배우
after school 방과 후
European 유럽 사람

다음 문장의 빈칸에 a(n)나 the를 쓰고, 필요 없으면 ×표 하세요.

1 I go to the hospital by _____ subway.

2 We want _____ apple and _____ peach.

3 There is a bear. Look at _____ bear!

4 _____ Ann is kind. I like Ann.

5 They have _____ lunch at 12:30.

6 _____ S(s)un rises in _____ east.

7 This is _____ Judy. She is _____ angel.

8 He is _____ honest boy.

9 I like _____ math and _____ English.

10 You want _____ orange.

11 This is _____ my umbrella.

12 They play _____ piano everyday.

13 There are many stars in _____ sky.

14 We play _____ basketball in the park.

15 I have _____ black jacket.

16 We have a test on _____ Thursday.

hospital 병원

peach 복숭아

bear 곰

kind 친절한

rise 떠오르다

star 별

jacket 재킷

test 시험

 Jump Up **1**

다음 빈칸에 알맞은 말을 쓰세요.

1 관사란 명사 앞에 붙는 말로 관사에는 부정관사 _____, _____과 정관사 _____가 있다. 대부분의 명사 앞에는 **a**를 붙이지만, 셀 수 있는 명사가 하나이면서 첫소리가 _____ 'a, e, i, o, u'로 소리 나는 명사 앞에는 _____을 붙인다.

2 a, an을 붙이지 않는 경우는 **1.** _____명사, 복수 명사 앞(**a Seoul** ×, **a cats** ×), **2.** 셀 수 없는 _____ 앞(**a milk** ×, **a peace** ×), **3.** _____ 앞(**a my computer** ×) 이다. 이때, 명사가 둘 이상이면 명사의 _____형을 쓴다.

3 정관사 _____는 가리키는 대상이 정확히 무엇인지 알 수 있는 경우에 사용하며 _____명사를 제외한 모든 명사 앞에 붙을 수 있다.

4 a, an은 **1.** 실제로 _____인 것을 나타낼 때(=**one**), **2.** 막연한 어떤 것을 나타낼 때(≠**one**), **3.** _____라는 의미로 쓰일 때(= **per**) 명사 앞에 붙는다.

5 the는 **1.** 앞에 나온 _____가 다시 반복될 때, **2.** 서로 알고 있는 것을 가리킬 때, **3.** 세상에서 유일한 _____ 앞에(**the earth, the moon, the sky**), **4.** 강, 바다 이름이나 _____, 위치 앞에(**the East Sea, the west**), **5.** _____ 이름 앞에(**the piano, the violin**) 붙인다.

6 명사 앞에 관사를 쓰지 않는 경우는 **1.** 호칭으로 쓰일 때, **2.** _____ 이름 앞에(**soccer, tennis, baseball**), **3.** 식사, _____ 앞에(**breakfast, lunch, math, English**), **4.** 건물이 본래 _____으로 쓰일 때(**go to school** 학교(공부하러) 가다), **5.** by+_____을 나타낼 때(**by+bus**)이다.

다음 문장에서 밑줄 친 부분을 바르게 고쳐 쓰세요.

artist 화가
MP3 player
MP3 플레이어
north 북쪽
carrot 당근
eagle 독수리

1 She is <u>an</u> student. → _____

2 My mother is <u>a</u> artist. → _____

3 The earth goes around <u>a</u> sun. → _____

4 I drink <u>a</u> milk. → _____

5 They play <u>a</u> baseball. → _____

6 We are <u>a</u> children. → _____

7 I buy <u>a</u> MP3 player. → _____

8 There is <u>an</u> book in the box. → _____

9 They go to <u>a</u> north. → _____

10 This is <u>an</u> university. → _____

11 That is a car. <u>A car</u> is nice. → _____

12 I like <u>a</u> alligator. → _____

13 We study <u>a</u> English. → _____

14 Many clouds are in <u>a</u> sky. → _____

15 We have <u>a</u> onion and a carrot. → _____

16 There is <u>a</u> eagle in the tree. → _____

 Jump Up 3

다음 문장에서 밑줄 친 부분을 바르게 고쳐 쓰세요.

noon 정오
Japanese 일본어
salad 샐러드
meal 식사
south 남쪽
ax 도끼
big 큰

1 You teach a science. → _____

2 I go to the bed at 9:30. → _____

3 Open a window, please. → _____

4 We have a lunch at noon. → _____

5 An earth is round. → _____

6 They can speak the Japanese. → _____

7 I know a honest girl. → _____

8 We eat salad for the dinner. → _____

9 They play violin very well. → _____

10 I eat three meals the day. → _____

11 People go to a south. → _____

12 A airplane is in the sky. → _____

13 The boys like an English. → _____

14 There is a ax on the chair. → _____

15 A waiter, bring me some water. → _____

16 I have an orange. A orange is big. → _____

다음 괄호 안의 단어를 이용하여 문장을 완성하세요. 필요하면 a나 an, the와 함께 쓰세요.

1 We have bread for _____. (lunch)

2 I play _____ on Saturday. (guitar)

3 My favorite subject is _____. (math)

4 I have _____. (umbrella)

5 They want _____. (computer)

6 Look at _____. (sky)

7 I have an eraser. _____ is new. (eraser)

8 _____ is in the sky. (eagle)

9 We sail on _____. (East Sea)

10 They learn _____. (Korean)

11 We play _____ twice a week. (soccer)

12 It is windy. Close _____. (door)

13 They go to _____ on Sundays. (church)

14 We live on _____. (earth)

15 There is _____ in the kitchen. (onion)

16 This is _____ story. (interesting)

bread 빵

favorite
(가장) 좋아하는

subject 과목

eraser 지우개

sail 항해하다

Korean 한국어

twice 두 번

kitchen 부엌

interesting 재미있는

[1~2] 다음 중 명사 앞에 붙는 말이 다른 것을 고르세요.

1 ① ant ② university
③ octopus ④ umbrella

2 ① hour ② computer
③ teacher ④ watch

3 다음 중 명사 앞에 the가 들어갈 수 없는 것을 고르세요.
① moon ② guitar
③ south ④ soccer

4 다음 중 빈칸에 들어갈 말로 알맞은 것을 고르세요.

> This is a _____.

① window ② bears
③ ugly boy ④ Seoul

5 다음 중 관사의 사용이 올바른 것을 고르세요.
① an children ② a honest girl
③ an MP3 player ④ a my jacket

[6~7] 다음 중 밑줄 친 말이 잘못된 것을 고르세요.

6 ① I have a red umbrella.
② There are an ants.
③ I eat three meals a day.
④ It is a white chair.

7 ① You like the moon.
② I like the English.
③ We play the violin well.
④ Birds fly in the sky.

[8~10] 다음 중 밑줄 친 부분이 잘못된 것을 고르세요.

8 ① The sky is blue.
② Close the window.
③ They go to a bed at ten.
④ We go to the park by bus.

9 ① They play the piano.
② We play soccer on Sunday.
③ The earth goes around the sun.
④ I have the dinner at 7 o'clock.

10 ① We see an European there.
② Give me the salt, please.
③ I have an orange.
④ My brother is an actor.

11 다음 우리말과 같도록 괄호 안에서 알맞은 것을 고르세요.

> 나는 나의 친구들과 점심을 먹는다.

I have (a, the, ×) lunch with my friends.

[12~15] 다음 중 문장의 빈칸에 알맞은 것을 고르세요.

12

I study math for an hour _____ day.

① a   ② an   ③ the   ④ 필요 없음

13

The sun rises in _____ east.

① a   ② an   ③ the   ④ 필요 없음

14

We play _____ basketball in the park.

① a   ② an   ③ the   ④ 필요 없음

15

This is Sally. She is _____ angel.

① a   ② an   ③ the   ④ 필요 없음

16 다음 중 잘못된 부분을 고르세요.

① This ② is ③ a interesting ④ story.

[17~19] 다음 중 바르지 않은 문장을 고르세요.

17 ① Open the door, please.
② You teach a math.
③ The earth is round.
④ They can speak Korean.

18 ① People go to the east.
② Waiter, bring me water.
③ An airplane is in the sky.
④ I eat three meals the day.

19 ① We have salad for the lunch.
② I have an eraser.
③ There is an onion on the table.
④ They go to church on Sundays.

[20~22] 다음 밑줄 친 부분을 바르게 고쳐 쓰세요.

20 I play a guitar on Saturday.

→ _____

21 We live on a earth.

→ _____

22 They learn the science.

→ _____

[23~25] 다음 빈칸에 a, an, the 중 알맞은 것을 쓰세요.

23 There is _____ university in the city.

24 We want _____ apple and grapes.

25 I have a bike. _____ bike is new.

서술형 평가

1 Ann eats _____ every morning. (breakfast)

2 Eric is playing _____. (violin)

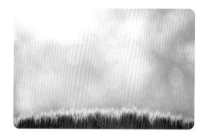

3 It is sunny. _____ is shining. (sun)

4 Boys play _____ after school. (soccer)

A: Is there _____ library on this street?

B: Yes, there is.

A: Where is _____ library?

B: Over there. It is next to the post office.

인칭대명사와 격변화

인칭대명사의 의미와 쓰임을 이해하고 활용할 수 있다.

인칭대명사의 격변화(주격, 목적격, 소유격)을 이해할 수 있다.

명사와 대명사의 일치를 이해하고 문장을 바꿀 수 있다.

대명사는 말 그대로 명사를 대신한다고 해서 대명사라고 해요. 대명사에는 인칭대명사, 지시대명사, 소유대명사가 있어요. 대명사를 사용하면 사람의 이름을 부르거나 사물을 지칭하지 않아도 간단하게 문장을 만들 수 있어서 경제적이에요.

Unit 5 인칭대명사와 격변화

1. 대명사

대명사는 말 그대로 명사를 대신한다고 해서 대명사라고 한다.

• 종류

(1) 인칭대명사: 사람을 대신해서 나타내는 대명사 I, you, he, she, it

(2) 지시대명사: 사물을 가리키는 대명사 this, that, these, those

(3) 소유대명사: 소유격＋명사를 대신하는 대명사 mine, yours

2. 인칭대명사

대신하는 대상에 따라 1, 2, 3인칭으로 나뉘며 둘 이상일 때는 복수형을 쓴다.

❶ 1인칭: 말을 하는 사람인 '나' 또는 나를 포함한 '우리'를 가리킨다.

❷ 2인칭: 말을 듣는 사람인 '너' 또는 '너희'를 가리킨다.

❸ 3인칭: 나와 너를 제외한 '나머지'나 '나머지들'을 가리킨다.

	1인칭	2인칭	3인칭		
단수	I 나	you 너	he 그	she 그녀	it 그것
복수	we 우리	you 너희	they 그들, 그것들		

I am a student. You are a student. 나는 학생이다. 너는 학생이다.

He is a doctor. She is a teacher. 그는 의사이다. 그녀는 선생님이다.

We are friends. They are friends. 우리는 친구들이다. 그들은 친구들이다.

It is a ruler. They are erasers. 그것은 자이다. 그것들은 지우개들이다.

3. 인칭대명사와 격변화

인칭대명사는 문장에서 주어, 목적어, 보어로 쓰이는데, 문장에서의 역할에 따라 주격, 목적격, 소유격으로 써야 한다.

	단수				복수			
	주격 (~은/는)	목적격 (~를)	소유격 (~의)	소유대명사 (~의 것)	주격 (~은/는)	목적격 (~를)	소유격 (~의)	소유대명사 (~의 것)
1인칭	I	me	my	mine	we	us	our	ours
2인칭	you	you	your	yours	you	you	your	yours
3인칭	he she it	him her it	his her its	his hers –	they	them	their	theirs

(1) 주격: 문장에서 주어 역할을 할 때 주격을 사용한다.

I am tall. You are smart. 나는 키가 크다. 너는 영리하다.

(2) 목적격: 문장에서 목적어 역할을 할 때, 목적격을 사용한다.

I like him. I like her. 나는 그를 좋아한다. 나는 그녀를 좋아한다.

(3) 소유격: 명사 앞에서 소유의 의미를 나타낼 때 사용한다.

It is my dog. It is your cat. 그것은 나의 개이다. 그것은 너의 고양이다.

(4) 소유대명사: 소유격＋명사로 '~의 것'이라는 뜻이다.

It is my bag. 그것은 나의 가방이다. ＝ The bag is mine. 그 가방은 나의 것이다.

I. 다음 중 목적격에 O표 하세요.

❶ I my me   ❷ he him his   ❸ them their theirs

4. 명사와 대명사의 일치

(1) 앞에 나온 명사를 뒤에서 다시 나타낼 때 대명사로 쓴다.

- 명사 단수형 → 대명사 단수형, 명사 복수형 → 대명사 복수형

  Kate is kind. She is a teacher. Kate는 친절하다. 그녀는 선생님이다.

- 명사 주격(목적격, 소유격) → 대명사 주격(목적격, 소유격)으로 쓴다.

  Ann is pretty. I know her. Ann은 예쁘다. 나는 그녀를 안다.

(2) 명사와 and로 연결된 말은 대명사의 복수형으로 쓴다.

1인칭 I와 함께 있으면 → we로 쓴다.	Eric and I are tall. We are tall.
2인칭 you와 함께 있으며 → you로 쓴다.	Jane and you are friends. You are friends.
3인칭 he, she, it과 함께 있으면 → they로 쓴다.	Dan and she are doctors. They are doctors.
명사 and 명사로 있으면 → they로 쓴다.	Sue and her brother are students. They are students.

5. 명사의 소유격

명사의 소유격과 소유대명사는 동일한 형태이다.

• 명사가 단수형: 명사 뒤에 –'s를 붙인다. Tom → Tom's bag Tom의 가방

• –s로 끝나는 복수형: '만 붙인다. boys → boys' school 남학교

• –s로 끝나지 않는 복수형: –'s를 붙인다. men → men's clothes 남자들의 옷

• 무생물 명사의 소유격: of+the 명사로 쓴다. a leg of the table 탁자의 다리

명사의 주격과 목적격은
문장에서 모양이 같다.
I like Joy. 나는 Joy을 좋아한다.

Pop Quiz

2. 다음 단어를 소유격으로 바꿔 쓰세요.

❶ my brother → _____ ❷ Sally → _____ ❸ boys → _____

다음 우리말에 해당하는 것을 골라 동그라미 하세요.

1 그녀를 (she, her, hers)

2 Ann은 (Ann, Ann's, of Ann)

3 그를 (he, his, him)

4 그녀의 것 (she, her, hers)

5 너를 (you, your, yours)

6 우리들을 (we, our, us)

7 나의 것 (my, me, mine)

8 그녀는 (her, she, hers)

9 그는 (he, his, him)

10 너의 (you, your, yours)

11 우리들의 것 (our, us, ours)

12 그의 것 (he, his, him)

13 그의 (he, his, him)

14 Ann의 (Ann, Ann's, of Ann)

15 그것은 (it, they, its)

16 그것들의 (they, their, them)

17 나의 (my, me, mine)

18 우리들은 (we, our, us)

19 나는 (I, me, mine)

20 그들은 (they, their, them)

21 그녀의 (she, her, hers)

22 우리들의 (we, our, us)

23 그것의 (it, their, its)

24 그것들을 (it, their, them)

25 너의 것 (you, your, yours)

26 그들의 (they, their, them)

27 그들의 것 (theirs, their, it)

28 나를 (I, me, mine)

29 너희의 것 (you, your, yours)

30 Ann을 (Ann, Ann's, of Ann)

다음 우리말은 영어로, 영어는 우리말로 쓰세요.

1	그녀를	_____	2	we _____
3	우리들을	_____	4	they _____
5	그를	_____	6	our _____
7	그들을	_____	8	mine _____
9	우리는	_____	10	him _____
11	나의	_____	12	he _____
13	너희들은	_____	14	she _____
15	그것은	_____	16	me _____
17	나의 것	_____	18	us _____
19	우리들의	_____	20	my _____
21	너희들을	_____	22	them _____
23	그녀의	_____	24	ours _____
25	그것의	_____	26	their _____
27	나를	_____	28	it _____
29	너의	_____	30	I _____

다음 괄호 안에서 알맞은 것을 골라 동그라미 하세요.

1   Put on (you, your, yours) shoes.

2   (We, Our, Us) like animals.

3   (I, My, Me) have a puppy.

4   I eat (she, her, hers) cookies.

5   (She, Her, Hers) has a boyfriend.

6   They know (he, him, his).

7   (He, His, Him) is late for school.

8   Nice to meet (you, your, yours).

9   Look at (he, his, him) robot.

10 (My, I, Me) father is very kind.

11 (It, Its, They) color is yellow.

12 He teaches (I, my, me) science.

13 Cows give (we, us, our) milk.

14 This is (my mother, my mother's) dress.

15 Happy is (I, my, mine) dog.

16 (You, Your, Yours) bag is on the table.

put on 입다
shoes 신발
animal 동물
puppy 강아지
cookie 쿠키
late 늦은
meet 만나다
teach 가르치다

다음 괄호 안에서 알맞은 것을 골라 동그라미 하세요.

camera 카메라
son 아들
clothes 옷
picture 그림, 사진
write 쓰다
letter 편지

1 (He, You, I) is a teacher.

2 This camera is (she, her, hers).

3 Tom and Peter like (mine, me, my).

4 (We, Our, Us) go to bed at ten.

5 She meets (he, his, him).

6 John and Dan are (she, her, hers) sons.

7 (They, Their, Theirs) have storybooks.

8 (Susan, Susan's) buys the clothes.

9 (She, Her, Hers) takes a picture.

10 This computer is (I, me, my, mine).

11 They are (you, your, yours) deer.

12 This is (Ashley, Ashley's) watch.

13 (It, Its, They, We) is my doll.

14 They are (the boy, the boy's) books.

15 The pigs are (we, our, us, ours).

16 (You, Your, Yours) write a letter.

다음 괄호 안에서 알맞은 것을 골라 동그라미 하세요.

tail 꼬리
short 짧은
cover 표지
have to ~해야 한다
run 달리다
bat 야구방망이
sleepy 졸린
sick 아픈

1 Judy likes music. (He, She, Her) listens to music.

2 This is a storybook. It is (my, me, mine).

3 The (dogs, dogs', dog's) tail is short.

4 Mom and dad is kind. I love (they, them, us).

5 I have a book. I read (it, its, it's) everyday.

6 I have a girlfriend. I like (him, her, our).

7 The cover (the book's, of the book) is blue.

8 There are pencils. They are (their, hers, my).

9 Ann and I are late. (We, I, You) have to run.

10 Tom likes baseball. This is (Toms, Tom's) bat.

11 Mark is (my, me, mine) friend. He is smart.

12 Mike and he are sleepy. (We, I, They) go to bed.

13 He is a mailman. I know (her, them, him).

14 His mom is a teacher. She teaches (us, our, ours).

15 The eraser is white. (They, He, It) is on the desk.

16 She and he are sick. (They, We, He) see a doctor.

다음 문장에서 밑줄 친 부분을 대명사로 바꾸어 쓰세요.

1 My mother cooks in the kitchen.   →   _____

2 Brian and I get up early.   →   _____

3 I like the storybook.   →   _____

4 Ann and Jamie have lunch.   →   _____

5 Look at the big elephants.   →   _____

6 I meet Julia at the library.   →   _____

7 They know Paul and you.   →   _____

8 Look at Jay and his dog.   →   _____

9 You help Tim in the evening.   →   _____

10 Jack and his wife are happy.   →   _____

11 My uncle is a vet.   →   _____

12 The building is near here.   →   _____

13 She teaches Amy and me math.   →   _____

14 The children go to school.   →   _____

15 Joe and I are close friends.   →   _____

16 The movies are interesting.   →   _____

cook
요리사, 요리하다
early 일찍
library 도서관
evening 저녁
vet 수의사
near 근처에
movie 영화

다음 밑줄 친 부분을 참고하여 빈칸에 알맞은 대명사를 쓰세요.

1 Billy and Jay play soccer. _____ are tired.

2 Jack and you are late. _____ have to hurry.

3 Hamsters are very small. _____ are cute.

4 My brother gets up. _____ has breakfast.

5 Look at the bears. _____ are sleeping.

6 I have a small camera. _____ is new.

7 Eric works in a restaurant. _____ is a cook.

8 Julia and Sue are friends. _____ are close.

9 Brian is my brother. _____ is very tall.

10 Sally and I like music. _____ listen to music.

11 The dog is very big. _____ eats so much.

12 I have many books. _____ are interesting.

13 John and you are sleepy. _____ go home early.

14 There are leaves. _____ are yellow.

15 The monkey likes bananas. _____ has long arms.

16 Ella and I are in the room. _____ study math.

tired 피곤한
hurry 서두르다
hamster 햄스터
get up 일어나다
restaurant 식당
cook 요리사, 요리하다
close 친한
arm 팔
room 방

Build Up 2

다음 괄호 안의 명사나 대명사를 알맞은 형태로 쓰세요.

1 They wash _____ hands. (they)

2 The pink skirt is _____. (Julia)

3 Boys fly _____ kites on the hill. (I)

4 _____ buy a new dictionary. (we)

5 The deer are _____. (I)

6 The crayons are _____. (my brother)

7 Mr. Smith helps _____ wife. (he)

8 _____ nose is very long. (it)

9 My mother knows _____. (he)

10 The scarf is _____. (she)

11 We remember _____. (you)

12 Tony and I meet _____ on Sunday. (Jenny)

13 Susan invites _____ to the party. (we)

14 _____ pants are blue. (you)

15 _____ uncle has a big truck. (she)

16 Mr. Brown teaches _____ English. (we)

skirt 치마

kite 연

hill 언덕

dictionary 사전

crayon 크레용

nose 코

scarf 스카프

remember 기억하다

invite 초대하다

truck 트럭

다음 문장을 소유대명사를 사용하여 바꿔 쓰세요.

1 It is his ruler.   → The ruler _____ is his _____.

2 They are your books.   → The books _____.

3 It is my robot.   → The robot _____.

4 They are her shoes.   → The shoes _____.

5 It is Molly's car.   → The car _____.

6 They are our dogs.   → The dogs _____.

7 It is my son's bike.   → The bike _____.

8 They are their bananas.   → The bananas _____.

9 It is her guitar.   → The guitar _____.

10 They are Mark's clothes.   → The clothes _____.

11 It is my sister's ball.   → The ball _____.

12 They are your chairs.   → The chairs _____.

13 It is his hat.   → The hat _____.

14 They are the children's boxes.   → The boxes _____.

15 It is Mark's apple.   → The apple _____.

16 It is my mother's knife.   → The knife _____.

다음 빈칸에 알맞은 말을 쓰세요.

1 대명사에는 사람을 대신하는 _____와 사람이나 사물을 가리키는 _____, 소유격+명사를 대신하는 _____가 있다.

2 인칭대명사에서 1인칭은 말하는 사람인 '____'와 '____'를, 2인칭은 듣는 사람인 '____'와 '너희'를, ____은 '나와 너를 제외한 나머지'를 의미한다. 또한 인칭대명사는 문장에서 _____, _____, 보어로 쓰이는데, 문장에서의 역할에 따라 주격, _____, _____으로 써야 한다.

3 인칭대명사의 격변화

	단수				복수			
	주격 (~은/는)	목적격 (~를)	소유격 (~의)	소유대명사 (~의 것)	주격 (~은/는)	목적격 (~를)	소유격 (~의)	소유대명사 (~의 것)
1인칭	I	_____	my	_____	_____	us	_____	ours
2인칭	_____	you	_____	yours	you	_____	your	_____
3인칭	he _____ it	_____ her it	_____ her _____	his _____	they	_____	their	_____

4 명사와 대명사의 일치

1인칭 I와 함께 있으면 → _____로 쓴다.	Eric and I are tall. → _____ are tall.
2인칭 you와 함께 있으면 → _____로 쓴다.	Jane and you are friends. → _____ are friends.
3인칭 he, she, it과 함께 있으면 → _____로 쓴다.	Dan and she are doctors. → _____ are doctors.
명사 and 명사로 있으면 → _____로 쓴다.	Sue and her brother are students. → _____ are students.

다음 문장에서 밑줄 친 부분을 바르게 고쳐 쓰세요.

1 Kate is <u>he</u> girlfriend. → _____

2 She is <u>Brian</u> mother. → _____

3 <u>Their</u> are fire fighters. → _____

4 The shoes are <u>your</u>. → _____

5 We are in front of <u>his</u>. → _____

6 The doctors help <u>she</u> everyday. → _____

7 <u>It</u> tail is long. → _____

8 Ella and <u>her</u> are wise. → _____

9 The toy car is <u>my brother</u>. → _____

10 They are <u>me</u> puppies. → _____

11 The pretty cap is <u>her</u>. → _____

12 <u>Dan</u> ducks are in the pond. → _____

13 There are sheep. Look at <u>they</u>. → _____

14 The children love <u>we</u>. → _____

15 The police officer knows <u>I</u>. → _____

16 They are <u>theirs</u> coins. → _____

fire fighter 소방관
in front of ~의 앞에
wise 현명한
cap (챙이 달린) 모자
duck 오리
pond 연못
police officer 경찰관
coin 동전

다음 괄호 안을 참고하여 빈칸에 알맞은 말을 쓰세요.

1   Peter likes books. _____ reads in the library. (he)

2   Mom and dad are short. _____ son is tall. (they)

3   I brush _____ teeth three times a day. (I)

4   We want pencils. Give _____ to us. (they)

5   I have a cat. _____ is my friend. (it)

6   It is cold. Put on _____ coat. (you)

7   There is a dog. The _____ tail is long. (dog)

8   They like the books. _____ are fun. (they)

9   I know Miller. _____ father is a doctor. (he)

10   I eat oranges. I like _____ most. (they)

11   Ashley is a nurse. She likes _____ job. (she)

12   You are a pretty girl. I like _____. (you)

13   I tell you. Listen to _____, please. (I)

14   Tom is kind. I go to the park with _____. (he)

15   This is a small tree. _____ leaves are green. (it)

16   The computer is new. It is _____ computer. (Tim)

library 도서관
brush 닦다
put on 입다
coat 코트
job 직업
listen 듣다

다음 우리말과 같도록 빈칸에 알맞은 인칭대명사를 쓰세요.

farmer 농부
pilot 조종사
parents 부모님
handsome 잘생긴
lawyer 변호사
delicious 맛있는

1 This is a toy. The toy is _____.

이것은 장난감이다. 그 장난감은 내 것이다.

2 _____ grandfather is a farmer.

그의 할아버지는 농부이다.

3 _____ know Susie. _____ is a pilot.

우리는 Susie를 안다. 그녀는 조종사이다.

4 The shoes are good. _____ likes _____.

그 신발은 좋다. 그는 그것들을 좋아한다.

5 _____ parents live in Seoul.

그들의 부모님은 서울에 산다.

6 Tom looks at _____. _____ loves her.

Tom은 그녀를 본다. 그는 그녀를 사랑한다.

7 I like _____. And I like _____, too.

나는 너를 좋아한다. 그리고 나는 그를 역시 좋아한다.

8 _____ is an elephant. _____ nose is long.

그것은 코끼리이다. 그것의 코는 길다.

9 Mr. Baker and _____ son help _____.

Baker 씨와 그의 아들이 그녀를 돕는다.

10 _____ teacher is very handsome.

우리 선생님은 매우 잘생겼다.

11 _____ grandmother is very old.

그들의 할머니는 매우 늙으셨다.

12 _____ sister is a lawyer. _____ brother is a vet.

나의 여동생은 변호사이다. 너의 남동생은 수의사이다.

13 There are potatoes. _____ are delicious.

감자들이 있다. 그것들은 맛있다.

14 Paul and Joe are _____ sons. I love _____.

Paul과 Joe는 나의 아들들이다. 나는 그들을 사랑한다.

[1~3] 다음 중 밑줄 친 부분이 잘못된 것을 고르세요.

1 ① I have a computer.
② She meets him.
③ I eat hers cookies.
④ Look at his robot.

2 ① This is my mother's skirt.
② Nice to meet your.
③ My teacher is very kind.
④ Your bag is on the chair.

3 ① This camera is her.
② Tom and John like me.
③ They have storybooks.
④ Susan buys the erasers.

[4~5] 다음 밑줄 친 부분을 대명사로 바꿀 때 알맞은 것을 고르세요.

4
> Peter and I get up early.

① We ② They
③ You ④ He

5
> My sister cooks in the kitchen.

① You ② He
③ We ④ She

[6~7] 다음 괄호 안에서 알맞은 것을 골라 동그라미 하세요.

6 The (cats, cats', cat's) tail is short.

7 The cover (the book's, of the book) is yellow.

[8~9] 다음 밑줄 친 부분을 대명사로 바꾼 것 중 틀린 것을 고르세요.

8 ① I meet Alice at the library.
　→ I meet her at the library.
② You help Tom in the evening.
　→ You help his in the evening.
③ Ann and Jane have lunch.
　→ They have lunch.
④ Look at the elephants.
　→ Look at them.

9　① She teaches <u>Tony and me</u> math.
　　　→ She teaches us math.
　　② <u>The children</u> go to school.
　　　→ They go to school.
　　③ <u>The building</u> is near here.
　　　→ Its is near here.
　　④ <u>Sally and I</u> are close friends.
　　　→ We are close friends.

12　① I have a cat. They is my friend.
　　② I eat bananas. I like them.
　　③ It is cold. Put on your jacket.
　　④ You are a pretty girl. I love you.

[13~14] 다음 우리말과 같도록 빈칸에 알맞은 말을 쓰세요.

13　그것은 코끼리다. 그것의 코는 길다.
　　_____ is an elephant. _____
　　nose is long.

[10~12] 다음 중 올바르지 <u>않은</u> 문장을 고르세요.

10　① She is Mark's mother.
　　② The children like we.
　　③ We are in front of him.
　　④ The doctor knows me.

14　그 옷은 좋다. 그는 그것들을 좋아한다.
　　The clothes are good. _____
　　likes _____ .

11　① Peter looks at her.
　　② Max and Eric are my sons.
　　③ Yours father is a vet.
　　④ Their parents live in London.

[15~16] 다음 문장에서 밑줄 친 부분을 바르게 고쳐 쓰세요.

15　The toy airplane is <u>my brother</u>.
　　→ _____

16 There are sheep. Look at they.

→ _____

[19~20] 다음 괄호 안에 주어진 낱말을 참고하여 문장의 빈칸에 알맞은 말을 쓰세요.

19 She and he are short. _____ son is tall.
(they)

[17~18] 다음 중 소유대명사를 사용하여 바꾼 것 중 <u>잘못</u> 바꾼 것을 고르세요.

17 ① It is my robot.

→ The robot is mine.

② It is Billy's car.

→ The car is Billy's.

③ It is her piano.

→ The piano is her.

④ They are our dogs.

→ The dogs are ours.

20 The bike is new. It is _____ bike.
(Tim)

18 ① They are your books.

→ The books are your.

② It is his cap.

→ The cap is his.

③ It is my brother's ball.

→ The ball is my brother's.

④ They are their apples.

→ The apples are theirs.

인칭대명사와 격변화 • **113**

A 다음 질문에 맞게 대명사를 사용하여 답해 보세요.

1 〈보기〉를 참고하여 친구와 함께 할 수 있는 것을 두 가지 쓰세요. (with를 사용하세요.)

> 〈보기〉 play soccer   ride the bikes   study math   swim in the pool

- _____

- _____

2 we와 us를 사용하여 문장을 만들어 보세요.

- _____ (we)

- _____ (us)

B 다음 그림을 보고, 대화의 빈칸에 알맞은 말을 쓰세요.

Susan's umbrella

Sandy: Is that your umbrella?

Susan: Yes, it's _____. I like red. (나의 것)

Amy's storybooks

Sandy: Are those _____ storybooks? (너의)

Susan: No. They are _____ storybooks. (Amy의)

Unit 6

지시대명사, 지시형용사

지시대명사의 의미와 쓰임을 이해할 수 있다.

지시형용사의 의미와 쓰임을 이해할 수 있다.

지시대명사와 지시형용사를 구별하고 활용할 수 있다.

지시대명사는 '이것(이 사람)', '저것(저 사람)'처럼 사물이나 사람을 가리키는 말로 명사를 대신해서 사용해요. 이때 주의해야 할 것은 지시대명사는 가까이 있을 때와 멀리 있을 때, 하나일 때와 여럿 일 때 모양이 달라져요. 또한, 지시형용사는 지시대명사와 형태는 같지만 역할은 달라 쓰임에 따라 구별해요.

Unit 6

지시대명사, 지시형용사

1. 지시대명사

지시대명사는 '이것(이 사람)', '저것(저 사람)'처럼 사물이나 장소, 사람을 가리키는 대명사로 모두 3인칭에 해당되며 be동사 is나 are와 함께 쓰인다.

	단수 명사	복수 명사
가까운 것을 가리킬 때	this(이것, 이 사람)	these(이것들, 이 사람들)
멀리 있는 것을 가리킬 때	that(저것, 저 사람)	those(저것들, 저 사람들)

- this: '이것(이 사람)'이라는 뜻으로 가까운 곳에 있는 단수를 가리킨다.
- that: '저것(저 사람)'이라는 뜻으로 멀리 있는 단수를 가리킨다.
- these: '이것들(이 사람들)'이라는 뜻으로 가까운 곳에 있는 복수를 가리킨다.
- those: '저것들(저 사람들)'이라는 뜻으로 멀리 있는 복수를 가리킨다.

This is a book.	That is a book.	These are books.	Those are books.
이것은 책이다.	저것은 책이다.	이것들은 책들이다.	저것들은 책들이다.

2. 지시형용사

this, that, these, those가 명사 앞에서 명사를 꾸며주는 형용사 역할을 할 때 this, that, these, those을 지시형용사라고 한다.

	+단수 명사	+복수 명사
가까운 것	this(이 ~)	these(이 ~들)
멀리 있는 것	that(저 ~)	those(저 ~들)

This is a kind man. 이 사람은 친절한 남자이다. [지시대명사]

This man is kind. 이 남자는 친절하다. [지시형용사]

That is an interesting book. 저것은 재미있는 책이다. [지시대명사]

That book is interesting. 저 책은 재미있다. [지시형용사]

Pop Quiz 1. 다음 괄호 안에서 알맞은 것을 고르세요.

❶ (This, These) is a bike. ❷ (That, Those) dogs are ours.

3. 지시대명사와 지시형용사의 차이점

- 지시대명사: 사물을 가리키는 대명사
- 지시형용사: 사물을 가리키는 형용사

지시대명사	지시형용사
사물을 가리키는 대명사 (주어, 목적어, 보어로 쓰인다.)	사물을 가리키는 형용사 (바로 뒤에 명사가 온다.)
this(이것) that(저것) these(이것들) those(저것들)	this+명사(이 ~) that+명사(저 ~) these+명사(이 ~들) those+명사(저 ~들)

4. 지시대명사, 지시형용사의 일치

this that	지시대명사	This is a ball. (○) 이것은 공이다. This are a ball. (×) This is balls. (×)
	지시형용사	This ball is mine. (○) 이 공은 나의 것이다. This ball are mine. (×) This balls are mine. (×)
these those	지시대명사	These are balls. (○) 이것들은 공들이다. These is balls. (×) These are a ball. (×)
	지시형용사	These balls are mine. (○) 이 공들은 나의 것들이다. These balls is mine. (×) These ball is mine. (×)

(1) 지시대명사의 일치

　→ this와 that은 is와 같이 쓰이며, these와 those는 are와 같이 쓰인다.

　→ This is[That is]＋단수 명사, These are[Those are]＋복수 명사가 온다.

(2) 지시형용사의 일치

　→ this[that]＋단수 명사,

　　these[those]＋복수 명사가 온다.

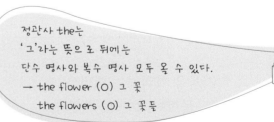

정관사 the는
'그'라는 뜻으로 뒤에는
단수 명사와 복수 명사 모두 올 수 있다.
→ the flower (○) 그 꽃
　 the flowers (○) 그 꽃들

Pop Quiz 2. 다음 밑줄 친 부분을 바르게 고쳐 쓰세요.

❶ These is trees.　→ _____

❷ This bags is yours.　→ _____

다음 주어진 말의 복수형을 골라 동그라미 하세요.

1	this box	(these box, these boxes)
2	that potato	(that potatoes, those potatoes)
3	that fork	(those forks, those fork)
4	this doctor	(these doctors, those doctors)
5	the dish	(the dishes, those dishes)
6	this radio	(this radios, these radios)
7	that coach	(those coach, those coaches)
8	this fox	(these foxes, these fox)
9	that child	(those children, these children)
10	the woman	(the women, these women)
11	this vase	(these vase, these vases)
12	this glass	(these glasses, these glass)
13	that spoon	(that spoons, those spoons)
14	the dress	(that dresses, the dresses)
15	that match	(those matches, these matches)
16	this flower	(these flowers, those flower)

fork 포크
coach 코치, 감독
vase 꽃병
spoon 숟가락
match 경기, 성냥

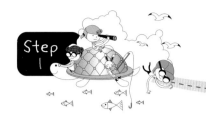

다음 주어진 말의 단수형은 복수형으로, 복수형은 단수형으로 고쳐 쓰세요.

ship 배
witch 마녀
song 노래
idea 생각, 개념
hippo 하마
jeep 지프차

1   this computer   → _____

2   those roofs   → _____

3   that sheep   → _____

4   the ships   → _____

5   that witch   → _____

6   this child   → _____

7   these fish   → _____

8   that song   → _____

9   this deer   → _____

10   the tomatoes   → _____

11   this idea   → _____

12   that hippo   → _____

13   this leaf   → _____

14   those jeeps   → _____

15   this candy   → _____

16   these mailmen   → _____

다음 주어진 말의 단수형은 복수형으로, 복수형은 단수형으로 고쳐 쓰세요.

1	those bags	→ _____
2	that dress	→ _____
3	this animal	→ _____
4	the principals	→ _____
5	these apples	→ _____
6	this piano	→ _____
7	those axes	→ _____
8	that movie	→ _____
9	these mice	→ _____
10	the wives	→ _____
11	those towers	→ _____
12	that restaurant	→ _____
13	this watch	→ _____
14	that eraser	→ _____
15	those queens	→ _____
16	these daughters	→ _____

principal 교장
movie 영화
tower 탑
restaurant 식당
queen 여왕
daughter 딸

다음 괄호 안에서 알맞은 것을 골라 동그라미 하세요.

rabbit 토끼
ear 귀
famous 유명한
expensive 비싼
interesting 재미있는
bean 콩
stamp 우표

1   (This, These) is a horse.

2   (This, Those) rabbits have long ears.

3   (That, These) hat is blue.

4   (This, These) are teachers.

5   (That, Those) artist is famous.

6   (This, These) is a nice watch.

7   (This, These) are my geese.

8   (That, These) tickets are expensive.

9   (This, Those) are her potatoes.

10 (That, Those) is an interesting book.

11 (That, Those) is a small dog.

12 (This, These) beans are green.

13 (This, These) is my friend, Jane.

14 (This, Those) letter is hers.

15 (That, Those) are stamps.

16 (This, These) girl is very pretty.

다음 밑줄 친 부분이 지시대명사이면 ○표, 지시형용사이면 △표 하세요.

garden 정원
hungry 배고픈
hairpin 헤어핀
lily 백합꽃
spider 거미
sweet 달콤한

1 <u>This</u> bag is expensive.   (   )

2 <u>That</u> is a beautiful flower.   (   )

3 <u>These</u> rooms are small.   (   )

4 <u>This</u> is Mr. White.   (   )

5 <u>Those</u> are my rulers.   (   )

6 <u>Those</u> bananas are yellow.   (   )

7 <u>That</u> cute cat is mine.   (   )

8 <u>These</u> are our tomatoes.   (   )

9 <u>Those</u> people are very kind.   (   )

10 <u>This</u> is a beautiful garden.   (   )

11 <u>Those</u> are hungry horses.   (   )

12 <u>Those</u> hairpins are ours.   (   )

13 <u>These</u> flowers are lilies.   (   )

14 <u>That</u> is a big spider.   (   )

15 <u>This</u> is my black jacket.   (   )

16 <u>Those</u> cookies are very sweet.   (   )

다음 그림을 보고, this(these)나 that(those)를 사용하여 완성하세요.

teddy bear 테디베어
(갈색 곰 인형)

photo 사진

delicious 맛있는

cookie 쿠키

bicycle 자전거

1

_____ is a cute teddy bear.

2

Look at _____ birds.

3

I like _____ photos.

4

_____ apples look delicious.

5

Take _____ umbrella.

6

_____ people are my friends.

7

_____ cookies are for you.

8

Jenny, _____ is Mark.

9

_____ is my bicycle.

10

_____ is my new bag.

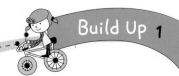

다음 주어진 우리말을 영어로 쓰세요.

melon 멜론
train 기차
dentist 치과의사
scientist 과학자

1 이 감자들 → _____

2 저 어린이 → _____

3 저 멜론들 → _____

4 이 기차 → _____

5 그 아기 → _____

6 이 호랑이 → _____

7 저 도시 → _____

8 이 양파들 → _____

9 저 사탕들 → _____

10 그 학생 → _____

11 이 나뭇잎들 → _____

12 저 치과 의사들 → _____

13 이 꽃 → _____

14 저 치마 → _____

15 이 과학자들 → _____

16 그 식당 → _____

다음 두 문장이 같은 뜻이 되도록 알맞은 것을 골라 동그라미 하세요.

palace 궁전
program 프로그램
glove 장갑
snake 뱀
dirty 더러운
really 정말

1 That is a small box.
= (Box that, That box) is small.

2 These are beautiful flowers.
= (These flowers, Flowers these) are beautiful.

3 That is a big palace.
= (That a palace, That palace) is big.

4 This is an interesting program.
= (This program, Program this) is interesting.

5 Those are delicious cookies.
= (Those cookies, Cookies those) are delicious.

6 These are red gloves.
= (These gloves are, Gloves are these) red.

7 This is a pretty woman.
= (This woman is, Woman this is) pretty.

8 That is a very long snake.
= (That is snake, That snake is) very long.

9 These are tall buildings.
= (These buildings are, These buildings is) tall.

10 Those are really dirty clothes.
= (Those clothes, That clothes) are really dirty.

다음 문장을 지시형용사를 사용하여 바꿔 쓰세요.

1 This is an interesting book.

→ _____

2 That is very fast ship.

→ _____

3 This is a delicious pumpkin.

→ _____

4 These are very smart boys.

→ _____

5 These are white bears.

→ _____

6 Those are colorful feathers.

→ _____

7 That is an expensive dish.

→ _____

8 This is an old picture.

→ _____

9 These are sharp knives.

→ _____

10 These are blue umbrellas.

→ _____

ship 배
pumpkin 호박
smart 영리한
feather 깃털
sharp 날카로운

다음 빈칸에 알맞은 말을 쓰세요.

1 _____대명사는 '이것(이 사람)', '저것(저 사람)'처럼 사물이나 장소, 사람을 가리키는 대명사로 모두 _____인칭에 속한다.

	단수 명사	복수 명사
가까운 것을 가리킬 때	_____ (이것, 이 사람)	_____ (이것들, 이 사람들)
멀리 있는 것을 가리킬 때	_____ (저것, 저 사람)	_____ (저것들, 저 사람들)

2 this, that, these, those가 명사 앞에서 명사를 꾸며주는 _____ 역할을 할 때, this, that, these, those을 _____형용사라고 한다.

	+단수 명사	+복수 명사
가까운 것	_____ (이 ~)	_____ (이 ~들)
멀리 있는 것	_____ (저 ~)	_____ (저 ~들)

3 지시대명사와 지시형용사의 차이점

지시대명사	지시형용사
사물을 가리키는 _____ (_____, 목적어, 보어로 쓰인다.)	사물을 가리키는 _____ (바로 뒤에 _____가 온다.)

4 지시대명사, 지시형용사의 일치

this that these those	지시_____	this와 that은 _____와 같이 쓰이며, these와 _____는 are와 같이 쓰인다. This[That] is+단수 명사, These[Those] are+복수 명사가 온다.
	지시_____	this[that]+단수 명사, these[those]+_____ 명사가 온다.

다음 문장에서 밑줄 친 부분을 올바르게 고쳐 쓰세요.

classroom 교실
dirty 더러운
hotel 호텔
thick 두꺼운
cousin 사촌
cheap (값) 싼
notebook 공책

1 These flower are for you. → _____

2 Those classroom is dirty. → _____

3 This hotels are expensive. → _____

4 This is new computers. → _____

5 Those is a thick book. → _____

6 Gloves these are blue. → _____

7 That are her keys. → _____

8 These woman is very tall. → _____

9 Those are my cousin. → _____

10 This watch are cheap. → _____

11 I like that pants. → _____

12 These are your notebook. → _____

13 That glasses are old. → _____

14 Those roofs is green. → _____

15 That child are in the park. → _____

16 These deer is very cute. → _____

다음 문장에서 밑줄 친 부분을 올바르게 고쳐 쓰세요.

famous 유명한
peacock 공작새
people 사람들
castle 성
heavy 무거운
ring 귀걸이

1 This shirts is yellow.   → _____

2 That hats are Brian's.   → _____

3 This are famous music.   → _____

4 These peacock are beautiful.   → _____

5 That are kind people.   → _____

6 Hamsters those are small.   → _____

7 That are an old castle.   → _____

8 These leaf are brown.   → _____

9 That bats are very heavy.   → _____

10 These is my toy cars.   → _____

11 That boys are my sons.   → _____

12 This vases is pretty.   → _____

13 Those rings is cheap.   → _____

14 This doctors is my father.   → _____

15 Those is his coacher.   → _____

16 This knives are sharp.   → _____

다음 우리말과 같도록 빈칸에 알맞은 인칭대명사를 쓰세요.

clever 똑똑한
grandfather 할아버지
strong 강한, 힘이 센
subject 과목
movie 영화
clean 깨끗한

1 _____ children are clever. 이 아이들은 똑똑하다.

2 _____ is my grandfather. 저분은 나의 할아버지다.

3 _____ are my notebooks. 이것들은 나의 공책들이다.

4 _____ man is very strong. 저 남자는 매우 힘이 세다.

5 I like _____ toy car. 나는 이 장난감 자동차가 좋다.

6 Wash _____ dishes, please. 저 접시들을 씻으세요.

7 _____ _____ my favorite subject.
   이것은 내가 가장 좋아하는 과목이다.

8 _____ _____ famous towers. 저것들은 유명한 탑들이다.

9 _____ _____ is black. 이 치마는 검정색이다.

10 _____ _____ a great movie. 저것은 멋진 영화이다.

11 _____ potatoes _____ very big. 이 감자들은 매우 크다.

12 _____ _____ white buildings. 저것들은 흰색 건물들이다.

13 _____ women _____ wise. 저 여자들은 현명하다.

14 _____ _____ is very tall. 이 나무는 매우 크다.

15 _____ _____ thick books. 이것들은 두꺼운 책들이다.

16 _____ room _____ clean. 저 방은 깨끗하다.

[1~2] 다음 중 단수형을 복수형으로 잘못 바꾼 것을 고르세요.

1
① the ship → the ships
② this deer → the deer
③ this computer → these computers
④ that witch → those witches

2
① that dress → those dresses
② this candy → these candies
③ that movie → those movies
④ this leaf → these leaf

3 다음 중 밑줄 친 this의 쓰임이 다른 것을 고르세요.
① <u>This</u> is an elephant.
② <u>This</u> is a nice bike.
③ <u>This</u> letter is yours.
④ <u>This</u> is a kind teacher.

[4~5] 다음 밑줄 친 부분의 단수형으로 알맞은 것을 고르세요.

4

<u>Those hippos</u> have big mouths.

① That hippo
② The hippo
③ This hippo
④ That hippos

5

These beans are brown.

① This beans
② This bean
③ These bean
④ The bean

[6~7] 다음 밑줄 친 부분이 지시대명사이면 ○표, 지시형용사이면 △표 하세요.

6 <u>That</u> cute dog is hers. (   )

7 <u>Those</u> are fast horses. (   )

[8~10] 다음 중 밑줄 친 부분의 쓰임이 다른 것을 고르세요.

8
① <u>This</u> skirt is expensive.
② <u>These</u> houses are small.
③ <u>Those</u> nurses are very kind.
④ <u>That</u> is his cute cat.

9
① <u>These</u> are our apples.
② <u>This</u> is a beautiful three.
③ <u>Those</u> hairpins are Jane's.
④ <u>That</u> is a big spider.

10
① <u>These</u> tickets are cheap.
② <u>That</u> is an interesting book.
③ <u>This</u> is a very brave boy.
④ <u>This</u> is my friend, Billy.

[11~12] 다음 문장에서 밑줄 친 부분을 올바르게 고쳐 쓰세요.

11 <u>Those roofs</u> is blue.

→ _____

12 <u>These are</u> a beautiful palace.

→ _____

[13~14] 다음 중 지시형용사를 사용한 문장으로 잘못 바꾼 것을 고르세요.

13 ① That is very fast train.

→ That train is very fast.

② These are blue hats.

→ This hats are blue.

③ Those are clean pants.

→ Those pants are clean.

④ These are very clever girls.

→ These girls are very clever.

14 ① That is an expensive radio.

→ That radio is expensive.

② These are new knives.

→ These knives are new.

③ This is an interesting program.

→ This program is interesting.

④ This is a delicious water melon.

→ The water melon is delicious.

[15~17] 다음 중 바르지 <u>않은</u> 문장을 고르세요.

15 ① Those river is dirty.

② This is an old photo.

③ Those flowers are colorful.

④ These bears are black.

16 ① These women are dentists.

② That children are in the park.

③ Those are my friends.

④ This car is expensive.

17 ① Those bags are very heavy.

② These are tall buildings.

③ This police officer is my father.

④ Those is my favorite subject.

[18~19] 다음 우리말과 같도록 빈칸에 알맞은 말을 쓰세요.

18 저것들은 오래된 탑들이다.

_____ _____ old towers.

19 이 어린이들은 현명하다.

_____ _____ are wise.

20 다음 빈칸에 들어갈 알맞은 말을 쓰세요.

These are sweet candies.

= _____ _____ are sweet.

A 다음 우리말과 같도록 빈칸에 알맞은 말을 쓰세요.

1 이 양말은 매우 따뜻하다.

→ _____ _____ are very warm.

2 이분은 나의 영어 선생님이다.

→ _____ _____ my English teacher.

3 저것들은 재미있는 만화책들이다.

→ _____ _____ interesting comic books.

B 다음 그림을 보고 질문에 맞게 this(these), that(those)를 사용하여 답해 보세요.

1 방에 있는 것을 가리키는 문장을 만들어 보세요.(지시대명사와 Brian's를 사용하여 두 문장을 쓰세요.)

• _____

• _____

2 위 두 문장을 지시형용사를 사용한 문장으로 바꾸어 보세요.

• _____

• _____

Unit 7

be동사의 현재시제

be동사의 의미와 쓰임을 이해할 수 있다.

be동사 현재시제의 긍정문을 이해하고 활용할 수 있다.

be동사는 직접 동작을 나타내지는 않지만, 주어의 성질이나 성격, 상태를 나타낼 때
사용해요. be동사에는 am, are, is가 있는데 주어에 따라 형태가 정해져 있으며,
모양은 서로 다르지만 '~이다', '~하다', '~이 있다'라는 뜻으로 모두같아요.

Unit 7

be동사의 현재시제

1. be동사란 무엇인가?

be동사는 직접 동작을 나타내지는 않지만, 주어의 성질이나 성격, 상태를 나타낼 때 사용한다.

• be동사에는 am, are, is가 있는데 주어에 따라 형태가 정해져 있다.

• 모양은 서로 다르지만 '~이다', '~하다', '~이 있다'라는 뜻으로 모두 같다.

I am a teacher. 나는 선생님이다. (be동사+명사 → ~이다)

You are smart. 너는 영리하다. (be동사+형용사 → ~하다)

He is on the sofa. 그는 소파에 있다. (be동사+장소, 위치 → ~에 있다)

2. 인칭대명사와 be동사

be동사 am, are, is는 문장 앞에 오는 주어에 따라서 결정되며 주어에 맞는 be동사가 정해져 있다.

• 주어: 동사의 주체가 되는 말로 문장의 맨 앞에 온다.

• 동사: 주어의 상태나 동작을 나타내는 말로 주어 다음에 온다.

	주어(단수)	be동사	축약형	주어(복수)	be동사	축약형
1인칭	I	am	I'm	We	are	We're
2인칭	You	are	You're	You		You're
3인칭	He She It	is	He's She's It's	They		They're

I am a student. 나는 학생이다.
I'm

We are students. 우리는 학생들이다.
We're

You are a student. 너는 학생이다.
You're

You are students. 너희는 학생들이다.
You're

She is a student. 그녀는 학생이다.
She's

They are student. 그들은 학생들이다.
They're

인칭대명사+be동사는 아포스트로피(')를 사용해서 줄여서 쓸 수 있다.

Pop Quiz

1. 다음 괄호 안에서 알맞은 것을 고르세요.

❶ He (am, are, is) a doctor.   ❷ We (am, are, is) friends.

3. 지시대명사와 be동사

주어에 지시대명사가 올 때, 단수이면 is를, 복수이면 are를 사용한다.

주어(단수)	be동사	축약형	주어(복수)	be동사	축약형
This	is	–	These	are	–
That		That's	Those		–

This is a book. 이것은 책이다.

That is a ball. 저것은 공이다.
That's

This is는 This's로 줄여 쓰지 않는다.

These are books. 이것들은 책들이다.

Those are balls. 저것들은 공들이다.

4. 명사와 be동사

(1) 셀 수 있는 명사: 주어에는 대명사만 오는 것이 아니라 명사도 올 수 있는데, 단수 명사는 is와 함께, 복수 명사는 are와 함께 쓰인다.

The child is smart. 그 어린이는 영리하다.

The children are smart. 그 어린이들은 영리하다.

(2) 셀 수 없는 명사: 단수 명사로 취급하기 때문에 is와 함께 쓰인다.

The cheese is white. 그 치즈는 흰색이다.

주어가 단수인 경우,
즉 단수 명사·셀 수 없는 명사이면 be동사 is와 함께 쓰고
주어가 복수인 경우,
즉 복수 명사·명사 and 명사이면 be동사 are와 함께 쓴다.

5. 복수형 문장만들기

• 단수형 주어와 동사를 복수형 주어와 동사로 모두 바꾼다.

• 이때, 주어가 명사인 경우에는 명사의 복수형으로 대명사인 경우에는 복수형 대명사로 바꾼다.

단수 주어(단수형)	am, are, is	단수 명사 / 형용사	
↓	↓	↓	↓
복수 주어(복수형)	are	복수 명사 / 형용사(변화 없음)	

This is **a ruler**. 이것은 자이다. → These are **ruler**s. 이것들은 자들이다.

He is **my friend**. 그는 나의 친구이다. → They are **my friend**s. 그들은 나의 친구들이다.

The car is **fast**. 그 차는 빠르다. → The cars are **fast**. 그 차들은 빠르다.

Pop Quiz **2.** 다음 괄호 안에서 알맞은 것을 고르세요.

❶ Amy (am, are, is) kind.   ❷ Time (am, are, is) money.

다음 괄호 안에서 알맞은 것을 골라 동그라미 하세요.

1 I (am, are, is) a student.

2 You (am, are, is) sick.

3 He (am, are, is) in the library.

4 She (am, are, is) so beautiful.

5 It (am, are, is) my computer.

6 We (am, are, is) close friends.

7 This (am, are, is) Brian's jacket.

8 Susie and I (am, are, is) teachers.

9 These (am, are, is) new televisions.

10 The question (am, are, is) difficult.

11 John (am, are, is) on the bus.

12 The leaves (am, are, is) green.

13 They (am, are, is) very angry.

14 That (am, are, is) an elephant.

15 Ann and Tom (am, are, is) brave.

16 He and she (am, are, is) very busy.

---

sick 아픈
close 친한
television 텔레비전
question 문제
difficult 어려운
angry 화난
brave 용감한
busy 바쁜

다음 괄호 안에서 알맞은 것을 골라 동그라미 하세요.

heavy 무거운
hungry 배고픈
genius 천재
enough 충분한
long 긴
soldier 군인, 병사

1 (That man is, That man are) kind.

2 (The boxes are, The boxes is) heavy.

3 (These is, These are) our bikes.

4 (The coffee is, The coffee are) sweet.

5 (This tiger is, This tiger are) hungry.

6 (The moon are, The moon is) round.

7 (This cars are, The cars are) expensive.

8 (Those apples are, The apples is) red.

9 (The boy is, The boy are) a genius.

10 (The cakes is, The cake is) on the table.

11 (These house is, These houses are) big.

12 (The water is, The water are) enough.

13 (That is, That are) my cute cat.

14 (Tony is, Tony are) very sleepy.

15 (The pencils is, This pencil is) long.

16 (His brother is, His brother are) a soldier.

다음 괄호 안에서 알맞은 것을 골라 동그라미 하세요.

1 (This building are, This building is) high.

2 His hands (am, are, is) small.

3 We (are engineer, are engineers).

4 (That are, That is) a yellow flower.

5 She is (a famous actress, famous actresses).

6 (The stars are, The stars is) bright.

7 These sweaters (is warm, are warm).

8 I (am, are, is) on the ladder.

9 This (is my wife, are their wives).

10 The photos (is wonderful, are wonderful).

11 (These dolls are, These dolls is) yours.

12 The boy (are my sons, is my son).

13 He (am, are, is) a very great cook.

14 Those men (are mailmen, is a mailman).

15 The office (is dirty, are dirty).

16 They (am, are, is) my cousin's balls.

high 높은
engineer 기술자
actress 여배우
bright 밝은
ladder 사다리
warm 따뜻한
wonderful 훌륭한

다음 밑줄 친 부분을 축약형으로 고치고, 고칠 수 없을 땐 ×표 하세요.

husband 남편
dancer 댄서
everyone 모든 사람
American 미국인
comic book 만화책

1 <u>You are</u> handsome. → _____

2 <u>She is</u> a nurse. → _____

3 <u>I am</u> her husband. → _____

4 <u>This is</u> your shirt. → _____

5 <u>He is</u> my grandfather. → _____

6 <u>You are</u> dentists. → _____

7 <u>Jacob is</u> a dancer. → _____

8 <u>We are</u> very busy. → _____

9 <u>It is</u> Judy's watch. → _____

10 <u>They are</u> Jenny's parents. → _____

11 <u>He is</u> kind to everyone. → _____

12 <u>That is</u> my school. → _____

13 <u>The book is</u> interesting. → _____

14 <u>Billy is</u> my brother. → _____

15 <u>She is</u> American. → _____

16 <u>This is</u> a comic book. → _____

다음 빈칸에 알맞은 am, are, is 중 알맞은 것을 쓰세요.

musician 음악가
hairdresser 미용사
full 배부른
Korean 한국인
soccer player
축구 선수

1 She _____ a musician.

2 They _____ in the classroom.

3 You _____ my best friend.

4 It _____ very tall.

5 They _____ clean.

6 Mr. Smith _____ a wise man.

7 The dogs _____ black.

8 Tom and Ashley _____ on the bench.

9 The new bag _____ expensive.

10 My aunt _____ a hairdresser.

11 Julie and you _____ full.

12 We _____ very tired.

13 A blue skirt _____ hers.

14 I _____ Korean. You _____ Canadian.

15 Huck _____ a soccer player.

16 Mark and I _____ late for school.

다음 문장의 빈칸에 알맞은 be동사를 쓰세요.

pianist 피아니스트
daughter 딸
astronaut 우주비행사
broken 깨진
pet 애완동물
strawberry 딸기
jam 잼

1   These _____ nice pants.

2   I _____ a pianist.

3   She _____ my daughter.

4   You _____ an astronaut.

5   They _____ big bears.

6   Jane and Alice _____ students.

7   That _____ a small hamster.

8   The windows _____ broken.

9   Those _____ their pets.

10 His feet _____ very dirty.

11 She and I _____ eleven years old.

12 The lady _____ my wife.

13 The strawberry jam _____ sweet.

14 Mom and dad _____ at home.

15 He _____ a good doctor.

16 These men _____ fire fighters.

다음을 복수형으로 만들 때, 괄호 안에서 알맞은 것을 고르세요.

store 가게
open 열려 있는
thief 도둑
fresh 신선한
raincoat 비옷, 우의

1 The store is open.

→ (The stores are, The stores is) open.

2 You are a scientist.

→ (They are, You are) scientists.

3 The house is on the hill.

→ (The houses are, The houses is) on the hill.

4 He is a farmer.

→ (He are, They are) farmers.

5 That man is a thief.

→ (Those men are, Those men is) thiefs.

6 She is a famous singer.

→ (They are, She are) famous singers.

7 He is my son.

→ They (is my sons, are my sons).

8 This carrot is fresh.

→ These carrots (are fresh, are freshes).

9 You are a gentleman.

→ You (are gentlemen, are gentlemans).

10 It is a raincoat.

→ They (are a raincoat, are raincoats).

다음 문장을 복수형 문장으로 바꿀 때, 빈칸에 알맞은 말을 쓰세요.

mp3 player
mp3 플레이어

over there 저 너머

healthy 건강한

1 This desk is very clean.

→ _____ very clean.

2 That mp3 player is Tom's.

→ _____ Tom's.

3 This is a dirty room.

→ These _____ .

4 That school is over there.

→ _____ over there.

5 She is a pretty girl.

→ They _____ .

6 This sofa is heavy.

→ _____ heavy.

7 That is a goose.

→ Those _____ .

8 It is a beautiful tower.

→ They _____ .

9 That flower is colorful.

→ _____ colorful.

10 The teacher is healthy.

→ _____ healthy.

다음 문장을 단수형 문장으로 바꿀 때, 빈칸에 알맞은 말을 쓰세요.

1 Those erasers are in my room

→ _____ in my room.

2 They are interesting books.

→ It _____ .

3 These puppies are very cute.

→ _____ very cute.

4 They are mailmen.

→ _____ mailman.

5 These bats are my friend's.

→ _____ my friend's.

6 Those carpenters are thirsty.

→ _____ thirsty.

7 These are light stones.

→ This _____ .

8 Those are small insects.

→ _____ small insect.

9 They are sweet melons.

→ It _____ .

10 You are his nephews.

→ _____ his nephew.

light 가벼운
carpenter 목수
thirsty 목이 마른
insect 곤충
nephew 조카

다음 빈칸에 알맞은 말을 쓰세요.

1 be동사에는 _____, _____, _____가 있는데 주어에 따라 형태가 정해져 있다.

2 인칭대명사와 be동사

	주어(단수)	be동사	축약형	주어(복수)	be동사	축약형
1인칭	I	_____	_____	We		_____
2인칭	You	_____	You're	You		_____
3인칭	He She It	_____	She's _____	They		They're

3 지시대명사와 be동사

주어에 지시대명사가 올 때, 단수이면 _____를, 복수이면 _____를 사용한다.

주어(단수)	be동사	축약형	주어(복수)	be동사	축약형
This	_____	–	These	_____	–
That		That's	Those		–

4 명사와 be동사

- 셀 수 있는 명사: 단수 명사는 _____와 함께, 복수 명사는 _____와 함께 쓰인다.
- 셀 수 없는 명사: 단수 명사로 취급하기 때문에 _____와 함께 쓰인다.

5 복수형 문장 만들기

- 단수형 주어와 동사 → 복수형 _____와 _____로 모두 바꾼다.

단수 주어(단수형)	am, are, is	단수 명사 / 형용사
↓	↓	↓ ↓
복수 주어(_____형)	_____	_____명사 / 형용사(변화 없음)

다음 문장에서 밑줄 친 부분을 바르게 고쳐 쓰세요.

post office 우체국
poor 불쌍한, 가난한
diligent 근면한
playground 운동장
money 돈

1 I <u>are</u> a good student. → _____

2 Sue and you <u>are singer</u>. → _____

3 They <u>is</u> in the post office. → _____

4 <u>This's</u> a white boat. → _____

5 <u>Those man</u> are honest. → _____

6 <u>We am</u> rich farmers. → _____

7 The puppies <u>is</u> in the house. → _____

8 <u>She'is</u> my close friend. → _____

9 You <u>is</u> a poor girl. → _____

10 Mark <u>are</u> very strong. → _____

11 <u>This women</u> are diligent. → _____

12 <u>Its</u> is a famous palace. → _____

13 He <u>are</u> on the playground. → _____

14 <u>Those train</u> is very fast. → _____

15 This is a <u>sweet melons</u>. → _____

16 Time <u>are</u> money. → _____

다음 문장을 단수형 또는 복수형 문장으로 바꾸어 쓰세요.

field 들판
player 선수
dolphin 돌고래
under ~ 아래에
sea 바다
peach 복숭아

1 These are Brian's computers.

→ _____

2 That boy is in the classroom.

→ _____

3 Those are your notebooks.

→ _____

4 The babies are very cute.

→ _____

5 My sister is in the room.

→ _____

6 This white house is mine.

→ _____

7 The cow is on the field.

→ _____

8 We are baseball players.

→ _____

9 That dolphin is under the sea.

→ _____

10 This peach is very delicious.

→ _____

다음 문장을 단수형 또는 복수형 문장으로 바꾸어 쓰세요.

wall 벽

kite 연

kitchen 부엌

1 He is a police officer.

→ _____ .

2 Those clocks are on the wall.

→ _____ .

3 This is a beautiful building.

→ _____ .

4 Those men are my teachers.

→ _____ .

5 That deer is under the tree.

→ _____ .

6 The woman is tall and pretty.

→ _____ .

7 You are a good pianist.

→ _____ .

8 These oranges are fresh.

→ _____ .

9 This kite is in the sky.

→ _____ .

10 She is in the kitchen.

→ _____ .

1 다음 중 주어와 be동사의 연결이 <u>잘못된</u> 것을 고르세요.

① He – is ② You – are
③ I – am ④ We – is

[2~3] 다음 중 밑줄 친 부분이 알맞은 것을 고르세요.

2 ① Susie and I <u>am</u> doctors.
② Ann and Tom <u>is</u> clever.
③ He and she <u>are</u> very sleepy.
④ His brother <u>are</u> a carpenter.

3 ① The cheese <u>are</u> enough.
② This lion <u>are</u> hungry.
③ The question <u>is</u> easy.
④ The cakes <u>is</u> on the table.

[4~5] 다음 빈칸에 들어갈 말로 알맞은 것을 고르세요.

4

Those apples _____ green.

① am ② are
③ is ④ the

5

She is a famous _____.

① actress ② dentists
③ nurses ④ scientists

[6~7] 다음 문장의 밑줄 친 부분을 줄여서 문장을 다시 쓰세요.

6 <u>He is</u> my uncle.

→ _____

7 <u>You are</u> a kind man.

→ _____

[8~9] 다음 중 밑줄 친 부분을 바르게 줄여 쓴 것을 고르세요.

8

<u>They are</u> your parents.

① They'are ② They're
③ They's ④ They'ar

9

<u>That is</u> my house.

① That're ② That'is
③ That's ④ That'm

10 다음 빈칸에 is를 쓸 수 <u>없는</u> 것을 고르세요.
① Those men _____ mailmen.
② The photo _____ wonderful.
③ The office _____ clean.
④ She _____ a kind nurse.

[11~12] 다음 문장에서 밑줄 친 부분을 바르게 고쳐 쓰세요.

11 This <u>women</u> are smart.

→ _____

12 She <u>are</u> my daughter.

→ _____

[13~14] 다음 중 be동사의 쓰임이 <u>다른</u> 것을 고르세요.

13 ① It <u>is</u> very strong.
② The cats <u>are</u> black.
③ The computer <u>is</u> expensive.
④ We <u>are</u> on the bench.

14 ① Those <u>are</u> their pets.
② His hands <u>are</u> very dirty.
③ You <u>are</u> a good doctor.
④ That <u>is</u> a small hamster.

[15~17] 다음 중 바르지 <u>않은</u> 문장을 고르세요.

15 ① She is on the hill.
② That man is my teacher.
③ The woman are tall and pretty.
④ Those clocks are on the wall.

16 ① My sister is at home.
② We are a soccer player.
③ This white house is hers.
④ This bag is very expensive.

17 ① They are interesting books.
② He's my close friend.
③ That cook are thirsty.
④ It is a famous building.

[18~19] 다음 문장의 빈칸에 공통으로 들어갈 말을 쓰세요.

18
> They _____ farmers.
> These carrots _____ fresh.

→ _____

19
> That comic book _____ Tom's.
> The teacher _____ healthy.

→ _____

[20~21] 다음 문장을 복수형 문장으로 바꾸어 쓰세요.

20 This baby is very cute.

→ _____

21 He is a good pianist.

→ _____

A 다음 표를 보고, 빈칸에 알맞은 말을 쓰세요.

	Country	Age	Job
Kevin	England	10	student
Julie	Canada	12	student

I Julie _____ from Canada. Julie는 캐나다 사람이다.

2 Kevin _____ ten years old. Kevin은 10살이다.

3 Kevin and Julie _____ students. Kevin과 Julie는 학생들이다.

B. 다음 질문에 맞게 빈칸에 알맞은 말을 쓰세요.

I 다음은 Dan의 자기소개서이다. 빈칸에 알맞은 be동사를 쓰세요.

Let me introduce myself. My name ____ Dan. I ____ ten years old.
I ____ from Seoul, Korea. I ____ short, but my favorite sport ____
basketball. Brian and Fred ____ my friends. I like them.

2 위 내용을 바탕으로 Ann의 남동생 Tom을 소개하는 글을 완성하세요.

Let me introduce Ann's brother. His name ____ Tom. He ____ ten
years old. ____ ____ from Seoul, Korea. He ____ short, but ____
favorite sport ____ basketball. Brian and Fred ____ ____ friends. He
likes them.

Unit 8

be동사의 부정문, 의문문

be동사의 현재시제의 긍정문을 이해하고 활용할 수 있다.

be동사의 현재시제의 의문문을 이해하고 활용할 수 있다.

be동사의 현재시제의 의문문에 대답하는 방법을 이해할 수 있다.

'~이 아니다', '~에 있지 않다'라는 부정의 말이 들어간 문장을 부정문이라고 하며, '아니다'라는 뜻의 not을 am, are, is 다음에 붙여서 써요. 또한 궁금한 것이 있을 때 '~이니?'라고 물어보는 문장이 의문문인데, be동사를 주어 앞으로 가져가고 문장 맨 끝에 물음표를 붙여요.

Unit 8

be동사의 부정문, 의문문

1. be동사의 부정문 (1)

'~이 아니다', '~하지 않다', '~에 있지 않다'라는 말이 들어간 문장을 부정문이라고 한다.

• be동사의 부정문은 be동사 뒤에 not을 붙여서 만든다.

	주어	be동사+not	축약형	주어	be동사+not	축약형
1인칭	I	am not	–	We		
2인칭	You	are not	aren't	You	are not	aren't
3인칭	He She It	is not	isn't	They		

I am not a teacher. 나는 선생님이 아니다.

You are not[aren't] smart. 너는 영리하지 않다.

He is not[isn't] on the sofa. 그는 소파에 있지 않다.

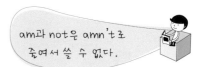

am과 not은 amn't로
줄여서 쓸 수 없다.

2. be동사의 부정문 (2)

주어	be동사+not	축약형	주어	be동사+not	축약형
This			These		
That	is not	isn't	Those	are not	aren't
단수 명사			복수 명사		

- 주어가 지시대명사일 때: this, that → is not / these, those → are not

  This is not[isn't] a book. 이것은 책이 아니다.

  Those are not[aren't] balls. 저것들은 공들이 아니다.

- 주어가 명사일 때: 주어가 단수명사 → is not / 복수명사 → are not

  The girl is not[isn't] tall. 그 소녀는 크지 않다.

  The children are not[aren't] sick. 그 어린이들은 아프지 않다.

Pop Quiz

1. 다음 괄호 안에서 알맞은 것을 고르세요.

   ❶ I (not am, am not) short.   ❷ He (isn't, aren't) a cook.

---

3. be동사의 의문문 (1)

궁금한 것이 있을 때 '~이니?'라고 물어보는 문장이 의문문이다.

- be동사 의문문: 주어와 be동사의 위치를 바꾸고 물음표를 붙인다.

  〈평서문〉 He is a student. 그는 학생이다.

  〈의문문〉 Is he a student? 그는 학생이니?

- 대답하기: 대답이 긍정이면 Yes를, 부정이면 No를 사용하여 답한다.

  Is he a doctor? 그는 의사니?   Yes, he is. 응, 그래.

  Is she tired? 그녀는 피곤하니?   No, she isn't. 아니, 그렇지 않아.

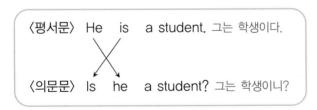

부정의 대답을 할 때는 주로 줄임말을 쓴다.

• 의문문의 주어가 1, 2인칭일 때는 대답의 주어가 달라진다.

의문문	긍정의 대답	부정의 대답
Am I ~? 내가 ~하니?	Yes, you are.	No, you aren't.
Are we ~? 우리가 ~하니?	Yes, you[we] are.	No, you[we] aren't.
Are you ~? 너는 ~하니?	Yes, I am.	No, I'm not.
Are you ~? 너희는 ~하니?	Yes, we are.	No, we aren't.

4. be동사의 의문문 (2)

• 주어가 지시대명사일 때

Is this a book? 이것은 책이니? – Yes, it is. / No, it isn't.

Are those balls? 저것들은 공들이니? – Yes, they are. / No, they aren't.

주어가 단수인 that, this인 경우 대답할 때는 it으로, 복수인 these, those인 경우 대답할 때는 they로 한다.

• 주어가 명사일 때

Is the boy tall? 그 소년은 키가 크니? – Yes, he is. / No, he isn't.

Are the horses fast? 그 말들은 빠르니? – Yes, they are. / No, they aren't.

주어가 단수명사인 경우 대답할 때는 he, she, it으로, 복수명사인 경우 대답할 때는 they로 한다.

 Pop Quiz 2. 다음 괄호 안에서 알맞은 것을 고르세요.

❶ (Am, Are, Is) she kind?　❷ (Am, Are, Is) those encils?

다음 밑줄 친 부분을 축약형으로 고치고, 고칠 수 없을 땐 ×표 하세요.

easy 쉬운
Japan 일본
boring 지루한
surprised 놀란

1　I am a student.　→ _____

2　No, he is not.　→ _____

3　This is not my pencil.　→ _____

4　Those are not my photos.　→ _____

5　The test is not easy.　→ _____

6　She is my aunt.　→ _____

7　The dishes are not on the table.　→ _____

8　We are not from Japan.　→ _____

9　They are Andrew's parents.　→ _____

10　No, you are not.　→ _____

11　These are not my clothes.　→ _____

12　This book is not boring.　→ _____

13　My house is not blue.　→ _____

14　They are not Jenny's books.　→ _____

15　He is not in the room.　→ _____

16　I am not surprised.　→ _____

다음 괄호 안의 단어를 바르게 배열하여 부정문을 만드세요.

apartment 아파트
fault 잘못
concert 콘서트
market 시장

1 She (not, is, a) good singer.

→ _____

2 This (not, our, is) apartment.

→ _____

3 He (not, is, a) soccer player.

→ _____

4 (not , you, are) a good sister.

→ _____

5 (not, is, it) your fault.

→ _____

6 The concert (not, is, good).

→ _____

7 Her (is, not, mother) in the market.

→ _____

8 Ann and (Tom, not, are) ten years old.

→ _____

9 They (are, not, in) the classroom.

→ _____

10 These (are, not, pictures) Vicky's.

→ _____

다음 주어진 단어들을 바르게 배열하여 의문문을 만드세요.

1 From Canada / David / is / ? David는 캐나다 사람이니?

→ _____

2 the woman / is / his teacher / ? 그 여자가 그의 선생님이니?

→ _____

3 are / Eric's keys / they / ? 그것들은 Eric의 열쇠들이니?

→ _____

4 Brian / is / late / today / ? Brian은 오늘 늦었니?

→ _____

5 your birthday / tomorrow / is / ? 너의 생일은 내일이니?

→ _____

6 ready / is / dinner / ? 저녁이 준비됐니?

→ _____

7 that gift / is / for her / ? 저 선물은 그녀를 위한 거니?

→ _____

8 are / baseball players / they / ? 그들은 야구 선수들이니?

→ _____

9 this man / your father / is / ? 이 남자가 너의 아버지시니?

→ _____

10 Jenny and Julia / are / sisters / your / ? Jenny와 Julia가 네 여동생들이니?

→ _____

다음 질문에 긍정은 Yes를, 부정은 No를 사용하여 대답을 쓰세요.

active 활동적인
insect 곤충
quiet 조용한
noisy 시끄러운
backpack 배낭

1 Is he clever? (긍정)   → _____

2 Are they hungry? (부정)   → _____

3 Are you active? (부정, 단수)   → _____

4 Is this an insect? (긍정)   → _____

5 Is it your computer? (부정)   → _____

6 Are the children quiet? (긍정) → _____

7 Is Billy in your house? (부정) → _____

8 Are these hot? (부정)   → _____

9 Are you sleepy? (긍정, 복수)   → _____

10 Is the box heavy? (긍정)   → _____

11 Are Tom and Dan strong? (부정) → _____

12 Is she a dentist? (부정)   → _____

13 Is Peter noisy? (긍정)   → _____

14 Is Jack a soccer player? (긍정) → _____

15 Is that his backpack? (부정)   → _____

16 Are they good actors? (긍정)   → _____

다음 문장을 부정문과 의문문으로 고쳐 쓰세요.(축약형을 쓰지 말 것)

1 She is ten years old.
(부정문) _____
(의문문) _____

2 This is your brother.
(부정문) _____
(의문문) _____

3 My socks are in the drawer.
(부정문) _____
(의문문) _____

4 He is interested in movies.
(부정문) _____
(의문문) _____

5 They are her students.
(부정문) _____
(의문문) _____

6 That soccer ball is yours.
(부정문) _____
(의문문) _____

7 Tony and Mark are in the classroom.
(부정문) _____
(의문문) _____

8 These paintings are beautiful.
(부정문) _____
(의문문) _____

drawer 서랍
interested 관심 있는
movie 영화
soccer ball 축구공
painting 그림

다음 질문에 대한 답을 쓰세요.(부정의 경우 축약형을 쓸 것)

suit 정장
baker 제빵사
lipstick 립스틱
lazy 게으른

1 Are these her flowers?

(긍정) _____

(부정) _____

2 Is that Brian's suit?

(긍정) _____

(부정) _____

3 Are Jane and Kate dentists?

(긍정) _____

(부정) _____

4 Is he a famous baker?

(긍정) _____

(부정) _____

5 Are they her students?

(긍정) _____

(부정) _____

6 Is this Jenny's lipstick?

(긍정) _____

(부정) _____

7 Is your sister lazy?

(긍정) _____

(부정) _____

8 Are those expensive clothes?

(긍정) _____

(부정) _____

다음 문장을 축약형을 사용하여 부정문으로 고쳐 쓰세요.

1 Her daughter is shy.

→ _____

2 My mother is in the bank.

→ _____

3 Sue and you are eleven years old.

→ _____

4 This exam is difficult.

→ _____

5 The giraffes are very tall.

→ _____

6 He is a great inventor.

→ _____

7 We are from China.

→ _____

8 That is a new bicycle.

→ _____

9 Judy and Ashley are roommates.

→ _____

10 The cute cat is on the sofa.

→ _____

shy 수줍어하는
bank 은행
exam 시험
giraffe 기린
inventor 발명가
roommate 룸메이트

다음 문장을 의문문으로 고쳐 쓰세요.

1 Her children are at school.

→ _____

2 You are a farmer.

→ _____

3 Your job is interesting.

→ _____

4 The stores are open today.

→ _____

5 It is dark outside.

→ _____

6 The station is near here.

→ _____

7 They are busy now.

→ _____

8 That young man is her cousin.

→ _____

9 His father is in the office.

→ _____

10 Paul and Jack are police officers.

→ _____

job 직업
today 오늘
dark 어두운
outside 밖에
station 역
busy 바쁜
now 지금
young 젊은

다음 〈보기〉를 참고하여 주어진 질문에 대답을 쓰세요.

ticket 티켓
alone 홀로
handsome 잘생긴

> Are those bags expensive?
>
> 〈보기〉 (긍정) Yes, they are. They are expensive.
>
> (부정 / cheap) No, they aren't. They are cheap.

1 Is this your ticket? (부정 / Daniel)

→ _____

2 Is Peter at home alone? (긍정)

→ _____

3 Are they dentists? (부정 / doctors)

→ _____

4 Are Tom and Tony tall? (부정 / short)

→ _____

5 Is that movie exciting? (긍정)

→ _____

6 Is this your pencil? (부정 / her)

→ _____

7 Are the children noisy? (부정 / quiet)

→ _____

8 Are those robots are Mark's? (긍정)

→ _____

9 Is Thomas handsome and tall? (긍정)

→ _____

다음 빈칸에 알맞은 말을 쓰세요.

Ⅰ be동사의 부정문

- be동사의 부정문은 be동사 뒤에 _____을 붙여서 만든다.

	주어(단수)	be동사+not	축약형	주어(복수)	be동사+not	축약형
1인칭	I	_____	-	We		
2인칭	You	_____	_____	You	are not	_____
3인칭	He She It	_____	isn't	They		

- 주어가 지시대명사일 때: this, that+_____ not / these, those+_____ not
- 주어가 명사일 때: 주어가 단수명사+_____ not / 복수명사+_____ not

2 be동사의 의문문

- be동사 의문문: _____와 _____의 위치를 바꾸고 물음표를 붙인다.
- 대답하기: 대답이 긍정이면 _____를, 부정이면 _____를 사용하여 답한다.
- 의문문의 주어가 1, _____인칭일 때는 대답의 주어가 달라진다.

의문문	긍정의 대답	부정의 대답
Am I ~? 내가 ~하니?	Yes, _____ are.	No, _____ aren't.
Are we ~? 우리가 ~하니?	Yes, you[_____] are.	No, you[_____] aren't.
Are you ~? 너는 ~하니?	Yes, I am.	No, I'm not.
Are you ~? 너희는 ~하니?	Yes, _____ are.	No, _____ aren't.

3 주어가 단수인 that, this인 경우에는 대답할 때 _____으로, 복수인 these, those인 경우에는 대답할 때 _____로 한다.

4 주어가 _____인 경우에는 대답할 때 he, she, it으로, _____인 경우에는 대답할 때 they로 한다.

다음 문장에서 밑줄 친 부분을 바르게 고쳐 쓰세요.

pencil case 필통
gentle 온순한
button 단추
rich 부유한

1 I not am a singer. → _____

2 Paul are not my brother. → _____

3 The window are not dirty. → _____

4 The boys isn't my sons. → _____

5 The pencil case aren't mine. → _____

6 That are not my house. → _____

7 She and I am not old friends. → _____

8 Is Tom and you hungry? → _____

9 Are James a nice boy? → _____

10 Are your horse gentle? → _____

11 Is this a button? – Yes, this is. → _____

12 Are they rich men? – Yes, he is. → _____

13 Is she sad? – No, they aren't. → _____

14 Are your sisters good? – Yes, she is. → _____

15 Is Jane sick? – No, she is. → _____

16 Are these books blue?
　　 – Yes, these are. → _____

다음에서 평서문은 의문문으로, 의문문은 평서문으로 고쳐 쓰세요.

windy 바람이 부는
violinist
바이올린 연주자
free 자유로운
basket 바구니

1 Your teacher is very kind.

→ _____

2 Are you all baseball players?

→ _____

3 Is Tom late for school?

→ _____

4 It is windy today.

→ _____

5 Is she a great violinist?

→ _____

6 These classrooms are quiet.

→ _____

7 They are free this afternoon.

→ _____

8 Are their son and daughter singers?

→ _____

9 Peter is handsome and tall.

→ _____

10 Are those your baskets?

→ _____

다음 우리말과 같도록 빈칸에 알맞은 말을 넣어 문장을 완성하세요.

French 불어
excellent 아주 훌륭한

1 이것은 John의 사무실이니?

→ _____ John's office?

2 Tom과 Ann은 집에 없다.

→ _____ at home.

3 그들은 친한 친구들이 아니다.

→ _____ close friends.

4 이 토마토들은 그 농부의 것이니?

→ _____ the farmer's?

5 Matt는 불어를 잘 하니?

→ _____ good at French?

6 그와 그의 개는 공원에 없다.

→ _____ in the park.

7 그들은 너의 부모님이시니?

→ _____ parents?

8 그는 아주 훌륭한 화가가 아니다.

→ _____ an excellent painter.

9 그 가수는 한국에서 유명하니?

→ _____ famous in Korea?

10 그 목걸이들은 너의 것이 아니다.

→ The necklaces _____

1 다음 문장에서 not이 들어가기에 알맞은 곳을 고르세요.

The ① notebooks ② are ③ on ④ the table.

[2~4] 다음 문장의 빈칸에 알맞은 말을 고르세요.

2

These _____ my pants.
이것들은 나의 바지가 아니다.

① is   ② aren't
③ are   ④ isn't

3

The test _____ difficult.
그 시험은 어렵지 않다.

① is   ② aren't
③ are   ④ isn't

4

Judy and Dan _____ ten years old. Judy와 Dan은 10살이 아니다.

① am   ② is
③ isn't   ④ aren't

[5~6] 다음 중 밑줄 친 부분이 잘못된 것을 고르세요.

5 ① This book <u>are not</u> boring.
② Tom <u>is not</u> a soccer player.
③ They <u>are</u> her parents.
④ <u>Is that</u> man his teacher?

6 ① That isn't our apartment.
② These pictures aren't Alice's.
③ You isn't a good brother.
④ She isn't a good actress.

7 다음 빈칸에 공통으로 알맞은 말을 고르세요.

· My socks _____ in the drawer.
· These paintings _____ beautiful.

① am   ② is
③ isn't   ④ aren't

[8~10] 다음 의문문에 대한 대답으로 알맞은 것을 고르세요.

8

Is Thomas in the room?

① Yes, she is.
② Yes, he is.
③ No, you are.
④ No, they aren't.

9

Are Tony and Eric fast?

① No, they aren't.
② No, he isn't.
③ No, we aren't.
④ No, they are.

10

> Is this her backpack?

① Yes, this is.　② Yes, they are.
③ Yes, it is.　④ Yes, it isn't.

[11~13] 다음 중 바르지 않은 문장을 고르세요.

11 ① Are they your students?
② Is this your father?
③ Is he eleven years old?
④ The children are noisy?

12 ① Her daughter isn't tall.
② The house aren't very big.
③ They aren't from Korea.
④ The cute dog isn't on the chair.

13 ① Are you a rich man? – Yes, I am.
② Is this a toy car? – Yes, this is.
③ Is she happy? – No, she isn't.
④ Are these roofs blue? – Yes, they are.

[14~15] 다음 대화의 빈칸에 알맞은 말을 고르세요.

14

> A: Is this your pencil?
> B: _____ It is his pencil.

① Yes, it is.　② Yes, they are.
③ No, they aren't.　④ No, it isn't.

15

> A: Is Brian handsome and tall?
> B: _____ He is handsome and tall.

① Yes, he is.　② Yes, you are.
③ No, he isn't.　④ No, you aren't.

16 다음 주어진 문장을 부정문과 의문문으로 고쳐 쓰세요.
Joseph is from America.
(부정문) → _____
(의문문) → _____

[17~18] 다음에서 틀린 부분을 찾아 ○표 하고, 고쳐 문장을 다시 쓰세요.

17 She and I am not in the park.
→ _____

18 Are Mark late for school?
→ _____

[19~20] 다음 우리말과 같도록 빈칸에 알맞은 말을 쓰세요.

19 이 감자들은 그 농부의 것이니?
→ _____ _____ _____ the farmer's?

20 그와 그의 개는 공원에 없다.
→ He and _____ _____ _____ in the park.

be동사의 부정문, 의문문 · **173**

A 다음 〈보기〉를 참고하여 주어가 바뀌었을 때, 알맞은 대답을 쓰세요.(주어의 성(남자, 여자), 수(단수, 복수), 인칭을 고려해서 be동사도 바꾸세요.)

〈보기〉 Is she tall? - Yes, she is. / No, she isn't.

의문문 주어	질문에 대한 대답	
	긍정	부정
I	Yes, you are.	
you(단수)		No, I'm not.
David(남자)		
Linda(여자)		
that		
mom and dad		
they		

B 다음 그림을 보고, 대화의 빈칸에 알맞은 말을 쓰세요.

Ann: Tom, are _____ in your room?

Tom: _____, I'm not. _____ _____ in the living room with my brother.

Ann: _____ he a student?

Tom: Yes, _____ _____. He is eight years old.

Memo

[1~2] 다음 밑줄 친 명사의 종류가 서로 같은 것을 고르세요.

1

> Matt is a teacher.

① I have a robot.
② We love Judy.
③ My family is large.
④ They are friends.

2

> I have a computer.

① Jane is my sister.
② I like coffee.
③ Give me some sugar.
④ This ball is mine.

[3~4] 다음 빈칸에 들어갈 수 없는 것을 고르세요.

3

> She is a _____.

① artist   ② cook
③ student   ④ singer

4

> This is an _____.

① umbrella   ② apple
③ university   ④ egg

5 다음 문장 중 어법상 어색한 것을 고르세요.
① I have three books.
② I need some sugar.
③ They are my childs.
④ James is an honest boy.

6 다음 중 밑줄 친 부분의 명사의 복수형이 잘못된 것을 고르세요.
① The leaves are green.
② They have two babys.
③ Birds have two feet.
④ You want many fish.

7 다음 중 문장의 빈칸에 a가 필요한 것을 고르세요.
① They are _____ close friends.
② My uncle is _____ doctor.
③ I like _____ milk.
④ That is _____ MP3 player.

[8~9] 다음 명사와 인칭대명사의 짝이 어색한 것을 고르세요.

8 ① Alice – she
② Tony and I – they
③ an eraser – it
④ my uncle and you – you

9 ① my teachers – they
② Mrs. Brown – she
③ Ann and Dan – they
④ my brothers – he

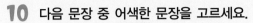

10 다음 문장 중 어색한 문장을 고르세요.

① She is my grandmother.

② You are ten years old.

③ They is my oxen.

④ Julia is my aunt.

[11~12] 다음 중 밑줄 친 부분이 잘못된 것을 고르세요.

11 ① <u>This is</u> my teacher.

② <u>That is</u> an expensive piano.

③ <u>Those are</u> your clothes.

④ <u>These is</u> big elephants.

12 ① <u>This boys</u> are my cousins.

② <u>This book</u> is interesting.

③ Look at <u>these pictures</u>.

④ <u>That puppy</u> is mine.

13 다음 문장에서 That의 뜻이 나머지와 다른 것을 고르세요.

① That is my kite.

② That is my friend, Jane.

③ That is green bag.

④ That is a big house.

[14~15] 다음 밑줄 친 부분의 대명사의 쓰임이 어색한 것을 고르세요.

14 ① Ashley is <u>his</u> student.

② <u>My</u> name is Jenny.

③ This is <u>our</u> house.

④ <u>Yours</u> bag is heavy.

15 ① I know <u>her</u>.

② Look at <u>us</u> bike.

③ <u>Her</u> dress is beautiful.

④ <u>He</u> is a smart child.

[16~17] 다음 문장을 괄호 안의 지시대로 고쳐 쓰세요.

16 The tomatoes are mine. (부정문)

→ _____

17 Jack's birthday is tomorrow. (의문문)

→ _____

[18~19] 다음 문장 중 자연스러운 것을 고르세요.

18 ① She not is my sons.

② These is not my rulers.

③ She is not an actress.

④ They not are from Japan.

19 ① She not is my sons.

② These is not my rulers.

③ She is not an actress.

④ They not are from Japan.

20 다음 주어진 질문에 대한 알맞은 대답을 고르세요.

> Are Max and Billy dentists?

① Yes, they are.　② Yes, he is.

③ No, we aren't.　④ No, they are.

1 다음 중 명사의 복수형을 만드는 방법이 <u>다른</u> 것을 고르세요.

① knife ② roof ③ leaf ④ wolf

2 다음 중 명사의 복수형이 <u>잘못된</u> 것을 고르세요.

① geese ② toys
③ leaves ④ oxes

[3~4] 다음 문장의 빈칸에 들어갈 수 있는 것을 고르세요.

3
> This is a _____.

① tiger ② milk
③ Seoul ④ salt

4
> I have a _____.

① orange ② sisters
③ mice ④ ruler

5 다음 중 This의 쓰임이 나머지와 <u>다른</u> 것을 고르세요.

① This camera is new.
② This skirt is black.
③ This is an old tower.
④ This boy is my son.

[6~7] 다음 우리말과 같도록 빈칸에 알맞은 말을 쓰세요.

6 _____ are pretty girls.

그들은 예쁜 소녀들이다.

7 He is _____ father.

그는 그녀의 아버지이다.

[8~9] 다음 중 밑줄 친 부분이 <u>잘못된</u> 것을 고르세요.

8 ① I have <u>two daughters</u>.
② Those <u>are buttons</u>.
③ The <u>potatoes</u> are big.
④ We have <u>five pencil</u>.

9 ① Men have <u>two hand</u>.
② I drink <u>a cup of tea</u>.
③ You have <u>an orange</u>.
④ <u>Many toys</u> are in the box.

10 다음 중 문장의 빈칸에 a가 필요한 것을 고르세요.

① I want _____ some bread.
② Give me _____ sheet of paper.
③ It is _____ interesting book.
④ She is _____ my cousin.

11 다음 중 인칭대명사의 변화형이 <u>잘못된</u> 것을 고르세요.

> 주격 – 목적격 – 소유격

① I – me – my
② we – us – our
③ she – her – hers
④ you – you – your

12 다음 문장의 빈칸에 들어갈 알맞은 인칭대명사를 고르세요.

> Look at _____ puppy.

① me　② he　③ us　④ her

13 다음 중 문장의 빈칸에 들어갈 말이 다른 것을 고르세요.

① My mom _____ a mailman.
② They _____ teachers.
③ Amy and Kate _____ kind.
④ The books _____ fun.

14 다음 중 밑줄 친 말의 쓰임이 나머지와 다른 것을 고르세요.

① I like these dolls.
② This is my uncle.
③ That flower is beautiful.
④ Those cars are cheap.

[15~16] 다음 문장 중 자연스러운 것을 고르세요.

15 ① These dog is big.
② This cups are yours.
③ That is your keys.
④ I like those pictures.

16 ① The cheese are white.
② My favorite food is milk.
③ That is your keys.
④ Judy and I am on the sofa.

17 다음 중 밑줄 친 부분이 자연스러운 것을 고르세요.

① These photos aren't mine.
② This isnot our apartment.
③ The stores isn't open now.
④ That test aren't easy.

18 다음 문장의 밑줄 친 부분의 뜻이 다른 것을 고르세요.

① They are my parents.
② You are a carpenter.
③ She is in the classroom.
④ Mark and Jane are singers.

[19~20] 다음 주어진 질문에 대한 알맞은 대답을 고르세요.

19

> Is your mother in the park?

① Yes, you are.
② Yes, we are.
③ No, they aren't.
④ No, she isn't.

20

> Is this your watch?

① Yes, it is.
② Yes, this is.
③ No, they aren't.
④ No, this isn't.

초등 영어 문법 실력 쌓기!

Grammar Builder

1

Answer Key

Answer Key

Unit 1 문장의 기본 구성

Pop Quiz

1. ❶ We – ○, are – △ ❷ They – ○, play – △
2. ❶ 평 ❷ 명 ❸ 의 ❹ 감
3. ❶ book ❷ very

■ Step 1 | Check Up 1   p. 21

1. flower, are, dog, tall, he, English, door, woman, doctor, father, teacher
2. He is not a teacher. He is tall. She is kind. I am a doctor.

■ Step 1 | Check Up 2   p. 22

1. They – ○, eat – △ 2. She – ○, is – △
3. We – ○, play – △ 4. They – ○, like – △
5. My mother – ○, is – △ 6. You – ○, are – △
7. my father – △ 8. soccer – ○ 9. cute – △
10. math – ○ 11. big – △ 12. the homework – ○

■ Step 1 | Check Up 3   p. 23

1. 평서문 2. 명령문 3. 감탄문 4. 평서문 5. 의문문
6. 감탄문 7. 명령문 8. 평서문 9. 의문문 10. 감탄문
11. 명령문 12. 의문문

■ Step 1 | Check Up 4   p. 24

1. 형용사 2. 대명사 3. 접속사 4. 명사 5. 전치사
6. 감탄사 7. 동사 8. 부사

■ Step 2 | Build Up 1   p. 25

1. V 2. C 3. O 4. S 5. O 6. S 7. V 8. C 9. O
10. V 11. S 12. V

■ Step 2 | Build Up 2   p. 26

1. 대, 동, 명 2. 명, 동, 형, 명 3. 동, 형, 명
4. 감, 대, 형 5. 동, 전, 명 6. 명, 접, 부, 형
7. 동, 명, 부 8. 명, 동, 전 9. 대, 동, 접, 명
10. 대, 형, 접, 동

■ Step 2 | Build Up 3   p. 27

1. 동사 2. 대명사 3. 형용사 4. 명사 5. 전치사
6. 부사 7. 명사 8. 동사 9. 부사 10. 접속사
11. 전치사 12. 감탄사

■ Step 3 | Jump 1   p. 28

1. 문장, 동사, 대문자, 마침표, 목적어, 보어
2. 평서문, 명령문 3. 단어, 품사, 8, 명사, 동사, 형용사, 동사, 형용사, 부사, 명사, 대명사, 시간, 접속사, 감탄사, 감정

■ Step 3 | Jump 2   p. 29

1. 명, 동, 명 2. 대, 동, 전, 명 3. 감, 명, 동, 부, 형
4. 대, 동, 명, 접, 명 5. 형, 명, 동, 전, 명
6. 명, 접, 대, 동, 형, 명 7. 대, 동, 명, 전, 명
8. 명, 동, 형, 명 9. 대, 동, 명, 부, 부
10. 명, 동, 전, 명

1. ③ 2. ① 3. ② 4. ② 5. ① 6. ③ 7. ③ 8. ②

9. ① 10. ② 11. ④ 12. ② 13. and 14. under

15. They − ○, play − △ 16. This − ○, is − △

17. a teacher − △ 18. milk − ○

19. The man is a doctor.

20. Are you a good student?

1. 여러 개의 단어들이 일정한 규칙에 따라 나열되어 하나의
   의미를 나타내는 것을 문장이라고 한다. 또한 문장은 주
   어와 동사가 있어야 한다.
2. 문장의 첫 글자는 항상 대문자로 쓴다.
3. 의문문의 문장 끝에는 물음표를 붙인다.
4. 다른 문장은 평서문이고 ②만 명령문이다.
6. my mother는 문장에서 보어이다.
7. small은 형용사, under는 전치사, teacher와 tiger,
   hospital은 명사, he는 대명사, eat는 동사, and는 접속
   사이다.
8. make와 study는 동사이다.
10. he, this, we는 대명사이고 Kate는 명사이다.
11. well, slowly, hard는 부사이고 to는 전치사이다.
12. buy, are, is는 동사이고 that은 대명사이다.
13. and는 '그리고, ~와'라는 뜻의 접속사이다.
14. under는 '~ 아래에'라는 뜻의 전치사이다.

A 1. beautiful flower, very beautiful flower
  2. A big cat, A big cat on the sofa
B 1. dog, big 2. on the chair, very well

A. 형용사는 명사를 꾸며주는 역할을 하며 명사 앞에 위치한
   다.

Unit 2 셀 수 있는 명사

Pop Quiz

1. book, family, student, team
2. ❶ dishes ❷ pianos

1. notebook, tree 2. apple, cat 3. student, chair

4. house, dog 5. computer, potato

6. tiger, doctor, family 7. woman, box, dish

8. window, bed 9. mouse, class

10. team, knife, boat 11. album, church

12. teacher, bike, bird 13. fish, picture

14. baby, roof, bus 15. bench, goose

16. ball, flower

1. dogs 2. maps 3. potatoes 4. families

5. men 6. feet 7. watches 8. leaves 9. pianos

10. lions 11. mice 12. sisters 13. benches

14. babies 15. children 16. books

1. cities 2. dishes 3. computers 4. boxes

5. oxen 6. tomatoes 7. radios 8. wolves

9. bags 10. dresses 11. sheep 12. monkeys

13. mothers 14. candies 15. roofs 16. fish

1. rulers 2. mailmen 3. butterflies 4. toys

5. classes 6. kids 7. desks 8. countries

9. wives 10. spoons 11. teams 12. trays

13. peaches 14. teeth 15. carrots 16. days

■ **Step 1** Check Up 5   p. 41

1. flies   2. lemons   3. parties   4. knives   5. feet
6. fish   7. benches   8. mailmen   9. roses
10. dresses   11. gentlemen   12. salmon
13. families   14. boys   15. hospitals   16. leaves

■ **Step 1** Check Up 6   p. 42

1. dogs, eggs, houses
2. cities, candies, families, ladies, babies
3. boys, toys, days
4. dishes, buses, potatoes, benches, boxes
5. pianos, radios, cellos
6. knives, wolves, leaves
7. roofs, chiefs

■ **Step 2** Build Up 1   p. 43

1. boxes   2. books   3. oxen   4. knives   5. feet
6. candies   7. bananas   8. classes   9. buses
10. tomatoes   11. kites   12. fish   13. mailmen
14. dragonflies   15. pianos   16. wives

■ **Step 2** Build Up 2   p. 44

1. roofs   2. watches   3. axes   4. robots
5. women   6. lemons   7. keys   8. thieves
9. balls   10. children   11. mice   12. foxes
13. deer   14. vases   15. cellos   16. dresses

■ **Step 2** Build Up 3   p. 45

1. dish   2. child   3. comedy   4. flag   5. goose
6. roof   7. mouse   8. deer   9. tomato   10. butterfly
11. classroom   12. ox   13. piano   14. country
15. watch   16. wolf

■ **Step 3** Jump 1   p. 46

1. 집합명사, 보통명사, 집합명사, 집합체
2. dogs, houses, es, buses, benches, boxes,
pianos, es, families, boys, toys, v, knives, roofs,
deer, teeth

■ **Step 3** Jump 2   p. 47

1. nurses   2. ladies   3. rulers   4. salmon   5. hats
6. peaches   7. chairs   8. fishermen   9. students
10. trays   11. radios   12. glasses   13. churches
14. monkeys   15. parties   16. matches

■ **Step 3** Jump 3   p. 48

1. geese   2. oxen   3. cities   4. toothbrushes
5. toys   6. deer   7. watches   8. pianos
9. children   10. dragonflies   11. mice   12. potatoes
13. policemen   14. museums   15. families
16. wolves

■ **Step 3** Jump 4   p. 49

1. mice   2. buses   3. children   4. apples   5. teeth
6. babies   7. dishes   8. flowers   9. foxes
10. deer   11. friends   12. leaves   13. dresses
14. roofs   15. buildings   16. women

■ **Step 4** 실전 평가   p. 50

1. ③   2. ②   3. ④   4. ①   5. ③   6. ①   7. ②   8. ④
9. ③   10. ③   11. ③   12. ②   13. ①   14. ②   15. ④
16. candies   17. ③   18. ④   19. ①   20. wolves
21. teeth   22. dresses   23. I see two policemen.
24. The dogs have four feet.
25. Five dishes are on the table.

1. gas는 눈에 보이지 않는 셀 수 없는 명사이다.
3. toy의 복수형은 -y에 s만 붙인 toys이다.
4. leaf의 복수형은 -f를 v로 바꾸고 es를 붙이는 형태로 leaves이다.
5. tooth의 복수형은 불규칙 변화로 teeth이다.
7. piano, radio, cello는 복수형을 만드는데, 예외 단어들로

-s만 붙여서 복수형을 만든다.

8. woman은 불규칙 변화로 복수형은 women이다.

9. salmon은 단수와 복수형이 같은 단어이다.

10. box의 복수형은 boxes, roof의 복수형은 roofs, sheep 의 복수형은 sheep이다.

12. 빈칸에는 단수형이 들어가야 하는데, children은 child 의 복수형이다.

15. 빈칸에는 명사의 복수형만 들어가는데, flowers는 flower의 복수형이다.

17. chair의 복수형은 chairs이다.

18. knife의 복수형은 knives이다.

19. 복수형 문장으로 단수 bench를 benches로 바꾸어야 한다.

■ Step 5 | 서술형 평가   p. 52

A **1.** roses, students, chairs / cities, ladies, families / knives, leaves, wolves

2. feet, children, deer – 불규칙 변화 복수형

B **1.** buses **2.** sheep **3.** teeth

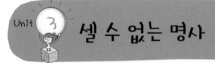

Unit 3 셀 수 없는 명사

Pop Quiz

1. 고유명사 – Seoul, Monday / 물질명사 – gold, rain, milk, salt, ink

2. ❶ cups ❷ bottle

■ Step 1 | Check Up 1   p. 57

1. air **2.** bread, rice **3.** April, war **4.** tea

5. paper, cheese **6.** time, music **7.** butter, gas

8. gold **9.** sand **10.** Jane **11.** Canada, sugar

12. love, Seoul **13.** salt **14.** juice, milk, math

15. Monday **16.** oil, wind

■ Step 1 | Check Up 2   p. 58

1. 물질명사 **2.** 고유명사 **3.** 물질명사 **4.** 물질명사

5. 추상명사 **6.** 고유명사 **7.** 추상명사 **8.** 추상명사

9. 물질명사 **10.** 물질명사 **11.** 고유명사 **12.** 고유명사

13. 추상명사 **14.** 물질명사 **15.** 고유명사 **16.** 물질명사

■ Step 1 | Check Up 3   p. 59

1. Tuesday, March, July, Korea, London, Seoul

2. sugar, milk, bread, snow, honey, sand, silver, soup

3. tennis, science, energy, hope, soccer, peace

■ Step 1 | Check Up 4   p. 60

1. cup **2.** glass **3.** bottle **4.** piece **5.** bowl

6. loaf **7.** sheet **8.** bunch **9.** pound **10.** bar

11. slice **12.** spoonful **13.** kilo **14.** bag **15.** glass

16. liter

■ Step 1 | Check Up 5   p. 61

1. slices **2.** bars **3.** flour **4.** kilos **5.** salt **6.** milk

7. pieces **8.** cups **9.** bowls **10.** ink **11.** liters

12. grapes **13.** slices **14.** bags **15.** paper

16. loaves

■ Step 1 | Check Up 6   p. 62

1. loaf **2.** shampoo **3.** sheets **4.** pieces

5. bananas **6.** bars, soap **7.** bottles

8. bags, rice **9.** piece **10.** cups, coffee

11. spoonfuls **12.** liter, juice **13.** bowls **14.** salt

15. kilo **16.** grapes

■ Step 2 | Build Up 1   p. 63

1. rain **2.** milk **3.** time **4.** water **5.** Seoul

6. love 7. Sunday 8. bread 9. cheese
10. sugar 11. Christmas 12. Jamie 13. sunshine
14. juice 15. White 16. hope

■ Step 2 | Build Up 2   p. 64

1. glass 2. pieces 3. pound 4. bottles 5. sheets
6. cup 7. spoonfuls 8. kilos 9. bunches
10. bowl 11. liters 12. bars 13. pieces 14. loaf
15. slices 16. bags

■ Step 2 | Build Up 3   p. 65

1. four bars of soap 2. two glasses of milk
3. five loaves of bread 4. two bottles of water
5. two bags of rice 6. three bunches of grapes
7. nine sheets of paper 8. three liters of juice
9. six pounds of flour 10. seven cups of coffee
11. four bowls of soup 12. three pieces of cake
13. two spoonfuls of oil 14. four kilos of sugar
15. two loaves of butter 16. eight pieces of pizza

■ Step 3 | Jump 1   p. 66

1. 이름, 고유명사, 물질명사, 추상명사, a, an, 복수형, 복
수형
2. a glass of water, 잉크 3병, a piece of cake, four
bowls of soup, 버터 2 덩어리, 종이 6장, five bags
of rice, 밀가루 1킬로, two liters of milk, a spoonful
of oil, 비누 4개, two pounds of sugar, a bunch
of grapes

■ Step 3 | Jump 2   p. 67

1. coffee 2. loaves 3. grapes 4. bottle 5. bars
6. pounds 7. bunches 8. sheet 9. meat
10. bars 11. spoonfuls 12. water 13. salad
14. bowls 15. sugar 16. loaf

■ Step 3 | Jump 3   p. 68

1. 종이 2장 2. 설탕 1파운드 3. 물 2잔
4. 버터 2 덩어리 5. 주스 5병 6. 케이크 3조각
7. 샐러드 4그릇 8. 소금 2 숟가락 9. 설탕 1킬로
10. 치즈 5조각 11. 커피 3잔 12. 오렌지주스 1잔
13. 피자 8조각 14. 우유 2리터 15. 초콜릿 6개
16. 바나나 2다발

■ Step 3 | Jump 4   p. 69

1. two pieces of bread 2. three kilos of flour
3. a piece of pizza 4. five cups of coffee
5. two bags of salt 6. four bottles of juice
7. six glasses of milk 8. two loaves of meat
9. a sheet of paper 10. three bottles of ink
11. four bars of chocolate 12. a spoonful of sugar
13. two bunches of grapes 14. five bowls of rice
15. a liter of water 16. three bowls of soup

■ Step 4 | 실전 평가   p. 70

1. ② 2. ④ 3. ③ 4. ① 5. ③ 6. ② 7. ① 8. ③
9. ④ 10. ② 11. bowls, salad 12. kilos, sugar
13. ③ 14. ② 15. ④ 16. bunch 17. ④ 18. ②
19. ① 20. bars 21. sheet 22. milk
23. three pieces of cheese
24. two pounds of flour 25. four bottles of milk

1. information은 셀 수 없는 명사 중 추상명사이다.
2. family는 셀 수 있는 명사 중 집합명사이다.
3. advice는 추상명사, grapes는 보통명사, New York는
고유명사이다.
4. juice는 물질명사, Christmas는 고유명사, flower는 보
통명사이다.
5. sunshine은 물질명사이다.
6. two loaves of butters로 물질명사는 복수형이 아닌 단
수형을 쓴다.
7. a glass of 는 ~ 한 잔이라는 뜻이다.
8. 비누는 a bar of를 사용하여 수량을 나타낸다.

9. 물질명사는 복수형을 만들 수 없으며 고유명사는 첫 글자를 대문자로 쓴다.

10. james를 James로 고쳐야 한다.

13. a bag of는 ~ 1봉지, a loaf of는 ~ 1 덩어리라는 뜻이다.

15. paper는 a sheet of를, chocolate은 a bar of를 사용한다.

17. meat는 물질명사로 복수형을 만들 수 없다.

18. two spoonfuls of salt로 단위에 복수로 나타내야 한다.

■ Step 5 | 서술형 평가   p. 72

A 1. Korea, Canada, Sunday, April / milk, water, sugar, paper / love, peace, math, soccer
2. bike, doctor, leaf – 셀 수 있는 명사
B 1. glass, pieces 2. juice, bowl, piece
3. cup, bunch

Unit 4 관사

Pop Quiz

1. ❶ a ❷ a ❸ an
2. ❶ × ❷ the ❸ ×

■ Step 1 | Check Up 1   p. 77

1. an 2. a 3. a 4. a 5. a 6. a 7. an 8. a 9. a
10. a 11. a 12. an 13. an 14. an 15. a 16. an
17. an 18. a 19. an 20. an 21. a 22. an 23. a
24. a 25. an 26. a 27. a 28. a 29. an 30. an

■ Step 1 | Check Up 2   p. 78

1. × 2. an 3. × 4. a 5. × 6. × 7. an 8. a
9. × 10. × 11. a 12. × 13. × 14. a 15. an
16. a 17. × 18. an 19. × 20. a 21. × 22. an
23. × 24. × 25. × 26. × 27. × 28. a 29. a
30. ×

■ Step 1 | Check Up 3   p. 79

1. a 2. × 3. × 4. an 5. × 6. a 7. × 8. an
9. × 10. × 11. an 12. a 13. × 14. × 15. a
16. an 17. × 18. × 19. × 20. an 21. × 22. an
23. a 24. × 25. an 26. an 27. × 28. a 29. an
30. ×

■ Step 1 | Check Up 4   p. 80

1. × 2. the 3. × 4. the 5. × 6. the 7. the
8. the 9. × 10. × 11. the 12. × 13. the 14. ×
15. the 16. ×

■ Step 1 | Check Up 5   p. 81

1. a 2. a 3. an 4. × 5. a 6. × 7. × 8. ×
9. a 10. × 11. × 12. a 13. × 14. ×, an
15. an, × 16. An, a

■ Step 1 | Check Up 6   p. 82

1. The 2. × 3. The 4. × 5. the 6. the 7. the
8. × 9. the 10. the 11. × 12. × 13. × 14. ×
15. × 16. the

■ Step 2 | Build Up 1   p. 83

1. × 2. the 3. The, the 4. × 5. × 6. The
7. × 8. × 9. the 10. × 11. the 12. ×
13. the, × 14. the 15. × 16. ×

■ Step 2 | Build Up 2   p. 84

1. an 2. the 3. a, The 4. × 5. a 6. an 7. The
8. × 9. an, a 10. × 11. the 12. an 13. the
14. × 15. a 16. the

■ Step 2 | Build Up 3 — p. 85

1. × 2. an, a 3. the 4. × 5. × 6. The, the
7. ×, an 8. an 9. ×, × 10. an 11. × 12. the
13. the 14. × 15. a 16. ×

■ Step 3 | Jump 1 — p. 86

1. a, an, the, 모음, an 2. 고유, 명사, 소유격, 복수
3. the, 고유 4. 하나, ~마다
5. 명사, 자연물, 방향, 악기
6. 운동, 과목, 목적, 교통수단

■ Step 3 | Jump 2 — p. 87

1. a student 2. an artist 3. the sun 4. milk
5. baseball 6. children 7. an MP3 player
8. a book 9. the north 10. a university
11. The car 12. an alligator 13. English
14. the sky 15. an onion 16. an eagle

■ Step 3 | Jump 3 — p. 88

1. science 2. bed 3. the window 4. lunch
5. The earth 6. Japanese 7. an honest girl
8. dinner 9. the violin 10. a day
11. the south 12. An airplane 13. English
14. an ax 15. Waiter 16. The orange

■ Step 3 | Jump 4 — p. 89

1. lunch 2. the guitar 3. math 4. an umbrella
5. a computer 6. the sky 7. The eraser
8. An eagle 9. the East Sea 10. Korean
11. soccer 12. the door 13. church 14. the earth
15. an onion 16. an interesting

■ Step 4 | 실전 평가 — p. 90

1. ② 2. ① 3. ④ 4. ① 5. ③ 6. ② 7. ② 8. ③
9. ④ 10. ① 11. × 12. ① 13. ③ 14. ④ 15. ②

---

16. ③ 17. ② 18. ④ 19. ① 20. the guitar
21. the earth 22. science 23. a 24. an 25. The

1. 첫소리가 모음 'a, e, i, o, u'로 소리 나는 명사 앞에는 an을 붙인다. 철자가 아닌 첫소리임에 유의한다.
3. 운동경기 이름 앞에는 the를 쓰지 않는다.
4. 복수명사, 고유명사 앞에는 부정관사 a/an을 쓰지 않는다.
5. 첫소리가 모음으로 발음되면 부정관사 an을 쓴다.
6. 복수명사 앞에는 부정관사가 올 수 없다.
7. 과목명 앞에는 관사가 붙지 않는다.
8. go to bed는 '잠자리에 들다(잠자다)'라는 뜻이다.
9. 식사 앞에는 정관사가 붙지 않는다.
12. '~ 마다'라는 뜻으로 per의 의미이다.
13. 방향이나 위치 앞에는 the가 붙는다.
16. interesting이 첫소리가 모음으로 발음되므로 an을 써야 한다.

■ Step 5 | 서술형 평가 — p. 92

A 1. breakfast 2. the violin 3. The sun 4. soccer
B a, the

Unit 5 인칭대명사와 격변화

Pop Quiz

1. ❶ me ❷ him ❸ them
2. ❶ my brother's ❷ Sally's ❸ boys'

■ Step 1 | Check Up 1 — p. 98

1. her 2. Ann 3. him 4. hers 5. you 6. us
7. mine 8. she 9. he 10. your 11. ours 12. his
13. his 14. Ann's 15. it 16. their 17. my 18. we

19. I 20. they 21. her 22. our 23. its 24. them
25. yours 26. their 27. theirs 28. me 29. yours
30. Ann

■ Step 1 | Check Up 2   p. 99

1. her 2. 우리는 3. us 4. 그(것)들은 5. him
6. 우리들의 7. them 8. 나의 것 9. we 10. 그를
11. my 12. 그는 13. you 14. 그녀는 15. it 16. 나를
17. mine 18. 우리들을 19. our 20. 나의 21. you
22. 그(것)들을 23. her 24. 우리들의 것 25. its
26. 그(것)들의 27. me 28. 그것은 29. your
30. 나는

■ Step 1 | Check Up 3   p. 100

1. your 2. We 3. I 4. her 5. She 6. him
7. He 8. you 9. his 10. My 11. Its 12. me
13. us 14. my mother's 15. my 16. Your

■ Step 1 | Check Up 4   p. 101

1. He 2. hers 3. me 4. We 5. him 6. her
7. They 8. Susan 9. She 10. mine 11. your
12. Ashley's 13. It 14. the boy's 15. ours
16. You

■ Step 1 | Check Up 5   p. 102

1. She 2. mine 3. dog's 4. them 5. it 6. her
7. of the book 8. hers 9. We 10. Tom's 11. my
12. They 13. him 14. us 15. It 16. They

■ Step 1 | Check Up 6   p. 103

1. She 2. We 3. it 4. They 5. them 6. her
7. you 8. them 9. him 10. They 11. He 12. It
13. us 14. They 15. We 16. They

■ Step 2 | Build Up 1   p. 104

1. They 2. You 3. They 4. He 5. They 6. It

7. He 8. They 9. He 10. We 11. It 12. They
13. You 14. They 15. It 16. We

■ Step 2 | Build Up 2   p. 105

1. their 2. Julia's 3. my 4. We 5. mine
6. my brother's 7. his 8. Its 9. him 10. hers
11. you 12. Jenny 13. us 14. Your 15. Her
16. us

■ Step 2 | Build Up 3   p. 106

2. are yours 3. is mine 4. are hers 5. is Molly's
6. are ours 7. my son's 8. are theirs 9. is hers
10. are Mark's 11. is my sister's 12. are yours
13. is his 14. are the children's 15. is Mark's
16. is my mother's

■ Step 3 | Jump 1   p. 107

1. 인칭대명사, 지시대명사, 소유대명사
2. 나, 우리, 너, 3인칭, 주어, 목적어, 목적격, 소유격
3. me, mine, you, your, she, him, his, its, hers, we,
   our, you, yours, them, theirs
4. we, We, you, You, they, They, they, They

■ Step 3 | Jump 2   p. 108

1. his 2. Brian's 3. They 4. yours 5. him
6. her 7. Its 8. she 9. my brother's 10. my
11. hers 12. Dan's 13. them 14. us 15. me
16. their

■ Step 3 | Jump 3   p. 109

1. He 2. Their 3. my 4. them 5. It 6. your
7. dog's 8. They 9. His 10. them 11. her
12. you 13. me 14. him 15. Its 16. Tim's

■ Step 3 | Jump 4   p. 110

1. mine 2. His 3. We, She 4. He, them 5. Their

6. her, He 7. you, him 8. It, Its 9. his, her
10. Our 11. Their 12. My, Your 13. They
14. my, them

■ **Step 4** | 실전 평가　　　　　　　p. 111

1. ③ 2. ② 3. ① 4. ① 5. ④ 6. cat's
7. of the book 8. ② 9. ③ 10. ② 11. ③ 12. ①
13. It, Its 14. He, them 15. my brother's 16. them
17. ③ 18. ① 19. Their 20. Tim's

1. '~을/를'에 해당하는 목적격이 와야 하며 she의 목적격은 her이다.
2. you의 목적격은 you이다.
3. '그녀의 것'이라는 뜻의 소유대명사가 와야 하며 she의 소유대명사는 hers이다.
5. 여자를 나타내므로 she가 된다.
6. 명사의 소유격은 명사 뒤에 –'s를 붙인다.
7. 무생물 명사의 소유격은 of+the 명사로 쓴다.
8. ②번에서 Tom은 목적격으로 쓰였으므로 인칭대명사 목적격을 써야 한다.
9. Its가 아닌 It을 써야 한다.
10. we의 목적격은 us로 we 자리에 us가 들어가야 한다.
11. you의 소유격은 your로 your father가 되어야 한다.
12. 사물이나 동물이 단수면 it으로, 복수면 they를 사용하여 나타낸다.
15. 명사의 소유대명사는 명사 뒤에 –'s를 붙인다.
16. they의 목적격은 them이다.
17. she의 소유대명사는 hers로 The piano is hers.가 되어야 한다.
18. you의 소유대명사 yours를 사용하여 The books are yours.가 되어야 한다.

■ **Step 5** | 서술형 평가　　　　　　p. 114

A 1. 예) I play soccer[study math] with my friends., I ride the bikes[swim in the pool] with them[her, him]. 등

2. 예) We go to the park., He teaches us English. 등

B mine, your, Amy's

Unit 6 지시대명사, 지시형용사

Pop Quiz

1. ❶ This ❷ Those
2. ❶ are ❷ bag

■ **Step 1** | Check Up 1　　　　　　p. 119

1. these boxes 2. those potatoes
3. those forks 4. these doctors 5. the dishes
6. these radios 7. those coaches 8. these foxes
9. those children 10. the women
11. these vases 12. these glasses
13. those spoons 14. the dresses
15. those matches 16. these flowers

■ **Step 1** | Check Up 2　　　　　　p. 120

1. these computers 2. that roof 3. those sheep
4. the ship 5. those witches 6. these children
7. this fish 8. those songs 9. these deer
10. the tomato 11. these ideas 12. those hippos
13. these leaves 14. that jeep 15. these candies
16. this mailman

■ **Step 1** | Check Up 3　　　　　　p. 121

1. that bag 2. those dresses 3. these animals

4. the principal 5. this apple 6. these pianos
7. that ax 8. those movies 9. this mouse
10. the wife 11. that tower 12. those restaurants
13. these watches 14. those erasers
15. that queen 16. this daughter

1. This 2. Those 3. That 4. These 5. That
6. This 7. These 8. These 9. Those 10. That
11. That 12. These 13. This 14. This 15. Those
16. This

1. △ 2. ○ 3. △ 4. ○ 5. ○ 6. △ 7. △ 8. ○
9. △ 10. ○ 11. ○ 12. △ 13. △ 14. ○ 15. ○
16. △

1. This 2. those 3. these 4. Those 5. this
6. Those 7. These 8. this 9. That 10. This

1. these potatoes 2. that child 3. those melons
4. this train 5. the baby 6. this tiger 7. that city
8. these onions 9. those candies 10. the student
11. these leaves 12. those dentists 13. this flower
14. that skirt 15. these scientists
16. the restaurant

1. That box 2. These flowers 3. That palace
4. This program 5. Those cookies
6. These gloves are 7. This woman is
8. That snake is 9. These buildings are
10. Those clothes

1. This book is interesting.
2. That ship is very fast.
3. This pumpkin is delicious.
4. These boys are very smart.
5. Those bears are white.
6. Those feathers are colorful.
7. That dish is expensive.
8. This picture is old.
9. These knives are sharp.
10. These umbrellas are blue.

1. 지시, 3, this, these, that, those
2. 형용사, 지시, this, these, that, those
3. 대명사, 주어, 형용사, 명사
4. 대명사, is, those, 형용사, 복수

1. These flowers 2. That classroom
3. These hotels 4. These are 5. That is
6. These gloves 7. Those are 8. This woman
9. That is 10. These watches 11. those
12. This is 13. Those glasses 14. That roof
15. Those children 16. This deer

1. This shirt 2. Those hats 3. This is
4. These peacocks 5. Those are
6. Those hamsters 7. That is 8. These leaves
9. Those bats 10. These are 11. Those boys
12. This vase 13. That ring 14. This doctor
15. That is 16. These knives

1. These 2. That 3. These 4. That 5. this

6. those **7.** This, is **8.** Those, are **9.** This, skirt
10. That, is **11.** These, are **12.** Those, are
13. Those, are **14.** This, tree **15.** These, are
16. That, is

■ **Step 4 ㅣ 실전 평가**   p. 132

1. ② **2.** ④ **3.** ③ **4.** ① **5.** ② **6.** △ **7.** ○ **8.** ④
9. ③ **10.** ① **11.** That roof **12.** This is **13.** ②
14. ④ **15.** ① **16.** ② **17.** ④ **18.** Those, are
19. These, children **20.** These, candies

1. this의 복수형은 these로 these deer로 써야 한다.
2. leaf의 복수형은 leaves로 these leaves가 되어야 한다.
3. this나 that 다음에 명사가 오면 이때는 지시대명사가 아닌 지시형용사이다.
4. those의 단수형은 that이고 hippos의 단수형은 hippo이다.
6. this나 that 다음에 동사가 오면 지시대명사이고 명사가 오면 지시형용사이다.
8. ④번은 지시대명사로 쓰였다.
11. be동사가 단수명사와 함께 쓰이는 is로 주어도 단수명사가 되어야 한다.
15. 명사가 river로 단수명사이고 동사도 is로 되어 있으므로 Those를 That으로 바꾸어야 한다.
16. children이 복수명사이므로 That을 Those로 바꾸어야 한다.

■ **Step 5 ㅣ 서술형 평가**   p. 134

A **1.** These, socks **2.** This, is **3.** Those, are
B **1.** 예) This is Brian's computer[Brian's bag]., Those are Brian's pants[Brian's gloves]. 등
   2. 예) This computer[bag] is Brian's., Those pants[gloves] are Brian's. 등

Unit 7 **be동사의 현재시제**

Pop Quiz
1. ❶ is ❷ are
2. ❶ is ❷ is

■ **Step 1 ㅣ Check Up 1**   p. 139

1. am **2.** are **3.** is **4.** is **5.** is **6.** are **7.** is
8. are **9.** are **10.** is **11.** is **12.** are **13.** are **14.** is
15. are **16.** are

■ **Step 1 ㅣ Check Up 2**   p. 140

1. That man is **2.** The boxes are **3.** These are
4. The coffee is **5.** This tiger is **6.** The moon is
7. The cars are **8.** Those apples are
9. The boy is **10.** The cake is
11. These houses are **12.** The water is
13. That is **14.** Tony is **15.** This pencil is
16. His brother is

■ **Step 1 ㅣ Check Up 3**   p. 141

1. This building is **2.** are **3.** are engineers
4. That is **5.** a famous actress **6.** The stars are
7. are warm **8.** am **9.** is my wife
10. are wonderful **11.** These dolls are
12. is my son **13.** is **14.** are mailmen **15.** is dirty
16. are

■ **Step 1 ㅣ Check Up 4**   p. 142

1. You're **2.** She's **3.** I'm **4.** × **5.** He's
6. You're **7.** × **8.** We're **9.** It's **10.** They're
11. He's **12.** That's **13.** × **14.** × **15.** She's
16. ×

1. is **2.** are **3.** are **4.** is **5.** are **6.** is **7.** are
8. are **9.** is **10.** is **11.** are **12.** are **13.** is
14. am, are **15.** is **16.** are

1. are **2.** am **3.** is **4.** are **5.** are **6.** are **7.** is
8. are **9.** are **10.** are **11.** are **12.** is **13.** is
14. are **15.** is **16.** are

1. The stores are **2.** You are **3.** The houses are
4. They are **5.** Those men are **6.** They are
7. are my sons **8.** are fresh **9.** are gentlemen
10. are raincoats

1. These desks are **2.** Those mp3 players are
3. are dirty rooms **4.** Those schools are
5. are pretty girls **6.** These sofas are
7. are geese **8.** are beautiful towers
9. Those flowers are **10.** The teachers are

1. This eraser is **2.** is an interesting book
3. This puppy is **4.** He is a **5.** This bat is
6. That carpenter is **7.** is a light stone
8. That is a **9.** is a sweet melon **10.** You are

1. am, are, is
2. am, I'm, are, is, He's, It's, are, We're, You're
3. is, are, is, are **4.** is, are, is
5. 주어, 동사, 복수, are, 복수

1. am **2.** are singers **3.** are **4.** This is
5. Those men **6.** We are **7.** are **8.** She's[She is]
9. are **10.** is **11.** These women **12.** It is
13. is **14.** trains are **15.** sweet melon **16.** is

1. This is Brian's computer.
2. Those boys are in the classroom.
3. That is your notebook.
4. The baby is very cute.
5. My sisters are in the room.
6. These white houses are mine.
7. The cows are on the field.
8. I am a baseball player.
9. Those dolphins are under the sea.
10. These peaches are very delicious.

1. They are police officers.
2. That clock is on the wall.
3. These are beautiful buildings.
4. That man is my teacher.
5. Those deer are under the tree.
6. The women are tall and pretty.
7. You are good pianists.
8. This orange is fresh.
9. These kites are in the sky.
10. They are in the kitchen.

1. ④ **2.** ③ **3.** ③ **4.** ② **5.** ① **6.** He's my uncle.
7. You're a kind man. **8.** ② **9.** ③ **10.** ①
11. These women **12.** is my daughter **13.** ④
14. ② **15.** ③ **16.** ② **17.** ③ **18.** are **19.** is
20. These babies are very cute.

21. They are good pianists.

1. we는 I의 복수형으로 be동사는 are와 함께 쓴다.
2. 명사와 명사, 명사와 대명사, 대명사와 대명사로 이어진 말은 여럿을 나타낸 복수형으로 are와 함께 쓴다.
4. 복수명사 주어는 be동사 are와 함께 쓴다.
5. 부정관사 a와 함께 쓰기 위해서는 단수명사가 와야 한다.
10. be동사 is는 단수 주어와 함께 쓰인다. 따라서 복수 주어 Those men과 함께 쓸 수 없다.
11. be동사 are가 있으므로 this를 these로 고쳐야 한다.
15. The woman은 be동사 is와 함께 쓴다.
16. 주어가 we인 것으로 보아 a soccer player를 soccer players로 바꾸어야 한다.
17. 단수명사 주어는 be동사 is와 함께 쓴다.

■ Step 5 | 서술형 평가   p. 154

A 1. is 2. is 3. are
B 1. is, am, am, am, is, are
   2. is, is, He, is, is, his, is, are, his

Unit 8   be동사의 부정문, 의문문

Pop Quiz

1. ❶ am not ❷ isn't
2. ❶ Is ❷ Are

■ Step 1 | Check Up 1   p. 159

1. I'm 2. isn't 3. isn't 4. aren't 5. isn't 6. She's
7. aren't 8. aren't 9. They're 10. aren't 11. aren't
12. isn't 13. isn't 14. They're 15. isn't 16. X

■ Step 1 | Check Up 2   p. 160

1. She is not a good singer.
2. This is not our apartment.
3. He is not a soccer player.
4. You are not a good sister.
5. It is not your fault. 6. The concert is not good.
7. Her mother is not in the market.
8. Ann and Tom are not 10 years old.
9. They are not in the classroom.
10. These pictures are not Vicky's.

■ Step 1 | Check Up 3   p. 161

1. Is David from Canada?
2. Is the woman his teacher?
3. Are they Eric's keys?
4. Is Brian late today?
5. Is your birthday tomorrow?
6. Is dinner ready?
7. Is that gift for her?
8. Are they baseball players?
9. Is this man your father?
10. Are Jenny and Julia your sister?

■ Step 1 | Check Up 4   p. 162

1. Yes, he is. 2. No, they aren't. 3. No, I'm not.
4. Yes, it is. 5. No, it isn't. 6. Yes, they are.
7. No, he isn't. 8. No, they aren't. 9. Yes, we are.
10. Yes, it is. 11. No, they aren't. 12. No, she isn't.
13. Yes, he is. 14. Yes, he is. 15. No, it isn't.
16. Yes, they are.

■ Step 1 | Check Up 5   p. 163

1. She is not ten years old., Is she ten years old?
2. This is not your brother., Is this your brother?
3. My socks are not in the drawer., Are my socks in the drawer?

4. He is not interested in movies., Is he interested in movies?

5. They are not her students., Are they her students?

6. That soccer ball is not yours., Is that soccer ball yours?

7. Tony and Mark are not in the classroom., Are Tony and Mark in the classroom?

8. These paintings are not beautiful., Are these paintings beautiful?

■ Step 1 ı Check Up 6   p. 164

1. Yes, they are., No, they aren't.
2. Yes, it is., No, it isn't.
3. Yes, they are., No, they aren't.
4. Yes, he is., No, he isn't.
5. Yes, they are., No, they aren't.
6. Yes, it is., No, it isn't.
7. Yes, she is., No, she isn't.
8. Yes, they are., No, they aren't.

■ Step 2 ı Build Up 1   p. 165

1. Her daughter isn't shy.
2. My mother isn't in the bank.
3. Sue and you aren't eleven years old.
4. This exam isn't difficult.
5. The giraffes aren't very tall.
6. He isn't a great inventor.
7. We aren't from China.
8. That isn't a new bicycle.
9. Judy and Ashley aren't roommates.
10. The cute cat isn't on the sofa.

■ Step 2 ı Build Up 2   p. 166

1. Are her children at school?
2. Are you a farmer? 3. Is your job interesting?
4. Are the shops open today?

5. Is it dark outside? 6. Is the station near here?
7. Are they busy now?
8. Is that young man her cousin?
9. Is his father in the office?
10. Are Paul and Jack police officers?

■ Step 2 ı Build Up 3   p. 167

1. No, it isn't. It is Daniel's ticket.
2. Yes, he is. He is at home alone.
3. No, they aren't. They are doctors.
4. No, they aren't. They are short.
5. Yes, it is. It is exciting.
6. No, it isn't. It is her pencil.
7. No, they aren't. They are quiet.
8. Yes, they are. They are his.
9. Yes, he is. He is handsome and tall.

■ Step 3 ı Jump 1   p. 168

1. not, am not, are not, aren't, is not, aren't, is, are, is, are
2. 주어, be동사, Yes, No, 2, you, you, we, we, we, we
3. it, they   4. 단수명사, 복수명사

■ Step 3 ı Jump 2   p. 169

1. am not 2. is not 3. is not 4. aren't 5. isn't
6. is not 7. are not 8. Are 9. Is 10. Is 11. it is
12. they are 13. she isn't 14. they are 15. isn't
16. they

■ Step 3 ı Jump 3   p. 170

1. Is your teacher very kind?
2. You are all baseball players.
3. Tom is late for school. 4. Is it windy today?
5. She is a great violinist.
6. Are these classrooms quiet?
7. Are they free this afternoon?

8. Their son and daughter are singers.

9. Is Peter handsome and tall?

10. Those are your baskets.

■ **Step 3 |** Jump 4　　　　　　　　　　p. 171

1. Is this　2. Tom and Ann are not[aren't]

3. They are not[aren't]　4. Are these tomatoes

5. Is Matt　6. He and his dog are not[aren't]

7. Are they your　8. He is not[isn't]

9. Is the singer　10. are not[aren't] yours.

■ **Step 4 |** 실전 평가　　　　　　　　　　p. 172

1. ③　2. ②　3. ④　4. ④　5. ①　6. ③　7. ④　8. ②
9. ①　10. ③　11. ④　12. ②　13. ②　14. ④　15. ①
16. am, Joseph is not[isn't] from America.,
　　Are, Is Joseph from America?,
17. She and I are not in the park.
18. Is Mark late for school?
19. Are, these, potatoes　20. his, dog, aren't

1. be동사의 부정문은 be동사 뒤에 not을 붙여서 만든다.

2. these는 be동사 are와 같이 쓰이며 are not은 aren't로 줄여서 쓸 수 있다.

3. 명사 단수 주어는 be동사 is와 같이 쓴다.

4. 명사 and 명사로 이루어진 주어는 복수로 be동사 are와 함께 쓴다.

6. you는 be동사 are와 함께 쓴다.

7. 명사 복수 주어는 be동사 are와 같이 쓴다.

8. be동사 의문문의 대답은 Yes나 No를 이용하여 답하며 의문문의 주어가 3인칭 남자인 경우에는 he를 사용하여 답한다.

9. 의문문의 주어가 복수인 사람인 경우에는 they를 사용하여 답한다.

10. 의문문의 주어가 사물 단수인 경우에는 it을 사용하여 답한다.

11. 의문문은 주어와 be동사의 위치를 바꾸고 맨 끝에 물음표를 붙인다.

17. She and I는 복수로 be동사 are와 함께 쓴다.

■ **Step 5 |** 서술형 평가　　　　　　　　　　p. 174

A No, you aren't., Yes, I am., Yes, he is., No, he isn't., Yes, she is., No, she isn't., Yes, it is., No, it isn't., Yes, they are., No, they aren't., Yes, they are., No, they aren't.

B you, No, I, am, Is, he, is

■ **Final Test 1**　　　　　　　　　　p. 176

1. ②　2. ④　3. ①　4. ③　5. ③　6. ②　7. ②　8. ②
9. ④　10. ③　11. ④　12. ①　13. ②　14. ④　15. ②
16. The tomatoes are not[aren't] mine.
17. Is Jack's birthday tomorrow?　18. ③　19. ③
20. ①

1. Matt, Judy처럼 사람 이름은 고유명사이다.

2. Jane은 고유명사, coffee와 sugar는 물질명사이다.

3. 첫 소리가 모음으로 발음이 나는 단어는 관사 an을 쓴다.

4. university는 글자는 모음이지만 자음으로 발음되어 관사 a를 쓴다.

5. child의 복수형은 children이다.

6. 단모음+y로 끝나는 단어는 y를 i로 바꾸고 -es를 붙인다.

7. 복수형과 물질명사에는 정관사 a/an을 붙이지 않는다.

8. Tony and I는 인칭대명사 we로 나타낸다.

9. 복수형은 인칭대명사 they로 나타낸다.

10. they는 be동사 are와 함께 쓰인다.

11. this와 that은 is와 these와 those는 are와 함께 쓰인다.

12. this와 that 다음에는 단수명사가, these와 those 다음에는 복수명사가 온다.

13. ②번은 사람을 소개하는 표현으로 '저 사람'이라는 뜻으로 쓰였다.

14. '~의'라는 뜻의 소유격 your가 되어야 한다.

15. 소유격이 와야 하므로 we이 소유격 our가 되어야 한다.

18. 부정문은 be동사+not으로 나타내며 주어에 맞는 be동사를 사용해야 한다.

20. Max and Billy는 they를 사용하여 나타낸다.

■ Final Test 2   p. 178

> **1.** ② **2.** ④ **3.** ① **4.** ④ **5.** ③ **6.** They **7.** her
> **8.** ④ **9.** ① **10.** ② **11.** ③ **12.** ④ **13.** ① **14.** ②
> **15.** ④ **16.** ② **17.** ① **18.** ③ **19.** ④ **20.** ①

1. -f(e)로 끝나는 명사의 복수형은 f(e)를 v로 바꾸고 -es를 붙인다. 예외적인 단어들이 있는데, roof는 roofs로 쓴다.

2. ox은 불규칙 변화로 복수형은 oxen이다.

3. 고유명사나 물질명사는 부정관사 a/an과 함께 쓰지 않는다.

4. 복수형 앞에는 부정관사 a/an을 쓰지 않는다.

5. this나 that이 명사 앞에 쓰이면 지시대명사가 아닌 지시형용사이다.

8. five pencils 또는 a pencil이라고 써야 한다.

10. ③번은 an interesting book으로 a가 아닌 an을 쓴다.

11. she의 소유격은 her이다.

12. '누구의 강아지'라는 뜻으로 '누구의'에 해당하는 소유격이 와야 한다.

13. 단수 주어는 be동사 is와, 복수 주어는 be동사 are와 함께 쓴다.

17. is not은 isn't로, are not은 aren't로 줄여서 쓸 수 있다.

18. be동사가 전치사 앞에 쓰이면 '~에 있다'라는 뜻이다.

19. your mother는 인칭대명사 she로 쓴다.

Memo

Memo

초등 영어 교재의 베스트셀러
초등 영어 문법 실력 쌓기!

Grammar Builder 1

Words in Grammar

Grammar Builder 시리즈

Grammar Builder 1
Grammar Builder 2
Grammar Builder 3
Grammar Builder 4
Grammar Builder 5

USA

You Are the Only One!

Iam books

doctor	의사	I am a doctor.	나는 의사이다.
teacher	선생님	He is a teacher.	그는 선생님이다.
kind	친절한	She is kind.	그녀는 친절하다.
tall	키가 큰	He is tall.	그는 키가 크다.
singer	가수	She is a singer.	그녀는 가수이다.
beautiful	아름다운	My mother is beautiful.	나의 어머니는 아름답다.
good	착한, 좋은	You are a good girl.	너는 착한 소녀이다.
soccer	축구	We play soccer.	우리는 축구를 한다.
learn	배우다	They learn math.	그들은 수학을 배운다.
homework	숙제	I do the homework.	나는 숙제를 한다.
police officer	경찰관	He is a police officer.	그는 경찰관이다.
close	닫다	Close the door.	문을 닫아라.
pretty	예쁜	She is very pretty!	그녀는 무척 예쁘구나!
open	열다	Open the window.	창문을 열어라.
tree	나무	What a tall tree it is!	그것은 정말 큰 나무구나!
wash	씻다	Wash your hands.	너의 손을 씻어라.
violin	바이올린	I can play the violin.	나는 바이올린을 연주할 수 있다.
sister	여자 형제	Your sister is a student.	너의 여동생은 학생이다.
tennis	테니스	I play tennis well.	나는 테니스를 잘 친다.
room	방	They are in the room.	그들은 방 안에 있다.
dinner	저녁 식사	We have dinner together.	우리는 함께 저녁을 먹는다.
elephant	코끼리	Elephants have big ears.	코끼리는 큰 귀를 가지고 있다.
bike	자전거	I buy a new bike.	나는 새 자전거를 산다.
table	탁자	The grapes are on the table.	그 포도는 탁자 위에 있다.
hard	열심히	They study math hard.	그들은 수학을 열심히 공부한다.
sad	슬픈	He is happy, but she is sad.	그는 행복하지만, 그녀는 슬프다.
smart	영리한	The girl is smart.	그 소녀는 영리하다.
box	상자	The doll is in the box.	그 인형은 그 상자 안에 있다.
juice	주스	I drink juice in the morning.	나는 아침에 주스를 마신다.
walk	걷다	They walk slowly.	그들은 천천히 걷는다.

church	교회	I go to church on Sunday.	나는 일요일에 교회에 간다.
picture	그림, 사진	There is a picture on the wall.	벽에 그림이 있다.
map	지도	This is a map.	이것은 지도이다.
watch	손목시계	I want a new watch.	나는 새 시계를 원한다.
city	도시	I live in this city.	나는 이 도시에 산다.
ox	황소	There are five oxen on the field.	들판에 5마리의 황소들이 있다.
radio	라디오	That is an old radio.	저것은 낡은 라디오이다.
mailman	우편배달부	He is an mailman.	그는 우편배달부이다.
peach	복숭아	I like peaches.	나는 복숭아를 좋아한다.
rose	장미	My favorite flower is a rose.	내가 가장 좋아하는 꽃은 장미이다.
hospital	병원	I go to the hospital.	나는 병원에 간다.
cello	첼로	I play the cello well.	나는 첼로를 잘 연주한다.
candy	사탕	I give him candies.	나는 그에게 사탕들을 준다.
kite	연	I have three kites.	나는 3개의 연을 가지고 있다.
mouse	쥐	She doesn't like a mouse.	그녀는 쥐를 좋아하지 않는다.
bus	버스	There are many buses on the road.	길에는 많은 버스들이 있다.
child	어린이	A child is playing with a doll.	한 어린이가 인형을 가지고 놀고 있다.
apple	사과	He buys a lot of apples.	그는 많은 사과들을 산다.
tooth	치아	The kid is brushing the teeth.	그 어린이는 양치질을 하고 있다.
baby	아기	She has three babies.	그녀는 3명의 아기가 있다.
dish	접시	There are some dishes.	약간의 접시들이 있다.
flower	꽃	Amy has many flowers.	Amy는 많은 꽃들을 가지고 있다.
fox	여우	The foxes are smart.	여우는 영리하다.
deer	사슴	There are five deer in the farm.	농장에는 5마리의 사슴이 있다.
friend	친구	They have a lot of friends.	그들은 많은 친구들이 있다.
leaf	나뭇잎	The leaves are falling.	그 잎들은 떨어지고 있다.
dress	드레스	Kate has a lot of dresses.	Kate는 많은 드레스를 가지고 있다.
roof	지붕	All the roofs are blue.	모든 지붕들이 파란색이다.
building	건물	Those are tall buildings.	저것들은 큰 건물들이다.
bench	벤치	A woman is on the bench.	한 여자가 벤치에 있다.

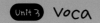
rain	비	I like rain.	나는 비를 좋아한다.
drink	마시다	We drink milk.	우리는 우유를 마신다.
time	시간	I need time.	나는 시간이 필요하다.
live	살다	They live in Seoul.	그들은 서울에 산다.
love	사랑	We want love.	우리는 사랑을 원한다.
bread	빵	I eat bread.	나는 빵을 먹는다.
know	알다	I know Mark.	나는 Mark를 안다.
visit	방문하다	I visit Mr. White.	나는 White 씨를 방문한다.
sunshine	햇빛	We need sunshine.	우리는 햇빛을 원한다.
hope	희망	They need hopes.	그들은 희망이 필요하다.
ink	잉크	They buy three bottles of ink.	그들은 잉크 3병을 산다.
want	원하다	I want four sheets of paper.	나는 종이 4장을 원한다.
oil	기름	I need two spoonfuls of oil.	나는 기름 2 숟가락이 필요하다.
flour	밀가루	We want two kilos of flour.	우리는 밀가루 2킬로를 원한다.
rice	쌀, 밥	We buy two bags of rice.	우리는 쌀 2봉지를 산다.
shampoo	샴푸	I want a bottle of shampoo.	나는 샴푸 1병을 원한다.
soap	비누	They have ten bars of soap.	그들은 비누 10개를 가지고 있다.
meat	고기	There are three loaves of meat.	고기 3 덩어리가 있다.
pepper	후추	We need two spoonfuls of pepper.	우리는 후추 2 숟가락이 필요하다.
butter	버터	I buy two loaves of butter.	나는 버터 2 덩어리를 산다.
salad	샐러드	I eat four bowls of salad.	나는 샐러드 4그릇을 먹는다.
salt	소금	They want two spoonfuls of salt.	그들은 소금 2숟가락을 원한다.
milk	우유	You drink a glass of milk.	너는 우유 1잔을 마신다.
chocolate	초콜릿	We need six bars of chocolate.	우리는 초콜릿 6개가 필요하다.
pizza	피자	I eat a piece of pizza.	나는 피자 1조각을 먹는다.
paper	종이	I want a sheet of paper.	나는 종이 1장을 원한다.
grape	포도	We have two bunches of grapes.	우리는 포도 2송이를 가지고 있다.
soup	수프	They eat three bowls of soup.	그들은 수프 3그릇을 먹는다.
sugar	설탕	I need a spoonful of sugar.	나는 설탕 1 숟가락이 필요하다.
cheese	치즈	You have two slices of cheese.	너는 치즈 2조각을 가지고 있다.

meal	식사	I eat three meals a day.	나는 하루에 3끼를 먹는다.
onion	양파	She has an onion.	그녀는 양파를 가지고 있다.
ax	도끼	This is my ax.	이것은 나의 도끼이다.
university	대학	There is a university in the town.	그 마을에 대학교가 있다.
tail	꼬리	An alligator has a long tail.	악어는 긴 꼬리를 가지고 있다.
moon	달	You like the moon.	너는 달을 좋아한다.
close	닫다	Close the window.	창문을 닫아라.
violin	바이올린	We play the violin well.	우리는 바이올린을 잘 연주한다.
west	서쪽	Tom and Eric go to the west.	Tom과 Eric은 서쪽으로 간다.
speak	말하다	I can speak English.	나는 영어를 말할 수 있다.
together	함께	They play soccer together.	그들은 함께 축구를 한다.
guitar	기타	Alice can play the guitar.	Alice는 기타를 연주할 수 있다.
everyday	매일	You play the cello everyday.	너는 매일 첼로를 연주한다.
ready	준비가 된	Breakfast is ready.	아침이 준비됐다.
mine	나의 것	The dog is mine.	그 개는 나의 것이다.
China	중국	We go to China by plane.	우리는 비행기로 중국에 간다.
cloud	구름	Look at the clouds in the sky.	하늘에 있는 저 구름을 봐라.
sea	바다	There are many fish in the sea.	바다에는 많은 물고기가 있다.
bring	가져오다	Waiter, bring me a cup of tea.	웨이터, 차 1잔 가져다 주세요.
album	앨범	This is an album.	이것은 앨범이다.
round	둥근	The moon is round.	달은 둥글다.
actor	배우	My father is an actor.	나의 아버지는 배우이다.
European	유럽 사람	We see a European.	우리는 유럽 사람을 본다.
rise	떠오르다	The sun rises in the east.	태양은 동쪽에서 뜬다.
angel	천사	She is an angel.	그녀는 천사이다.
jacket	재킷	I have a black jacket.	나는 검정색 재킷이 있다.
test	시험	We have a test on Thursday.	우리는 목요일에 시험이 있다.
artist	화가	My mother is an artist.	나의 어머니는 화가이다.
subject	과목	My favorite subject is math.	내가 가장 좋아하는 과목은 수학이다.
sail	항해하다	We sail on East Sea.	우리는 동해를 항해한다.

animal	동물	We like animals.	우리는 동물을 좋아한다.
puppy	강아지	I have a puppy.	나는 강아지를 가지고 있다.
cookie	쿠키	I eat her cookies.	나는 그녀의 쿠키를 먹는다.
late	늦은	He is late for school.	그는 학교에 늦는다.
camera	카메라	This camera is hers.	이 카메라는 그녀의 것이다.
son	아들	John and Dan are her sons.	John과 Dan은 그녀의 아들들이다.
write	쓰다	You write a letter.	너는 편지를 쓴다.
short	짧은	The dog's tail is short.	그 개의 꼬리는 짧다.
cover	표지	The cover of the book is blue.	그 책의 표지는 파란색이다.
run	달리다	We have to run.	우리는 달려야만 한다.
sleepy	졸린	Mike and I are sleepy.	Mike와 나는 졸립다.
sick	아픈	She and he are sick.	그녀와 그는 아프다.
early	일찍	Brian and I get up early.	Brian과 나는 일찍 일어난다.
library	도서관	I meet Julia at the library.	나는 Julia를 도서관에서 만난다.
vet	수의사	My uncle is a vet.	나의 삼촌은 수의사이다.
near	근처에	The building is near here.	그 빌딩은 여기 근처에 있다.
movie	영화	The movies are interesting.	그 영화들은 재미있다.
tired	피곤한	They are tired.	그들은 피곤하다.
hurry	서두르다	You have to hurry.	너는 서둘러야만 한다.
hamster	햄스터	Hamsters are very small.	햄스터들은 매우 작다.
restaurant	식당	Eric works in a restaurant.	Eric은 식당에서 일한다.
cook	요리사	He is a cook.	그는 요리사이다.
close	친한	They are close.	그들은 친하다.
room	방	Ella and I are in the room.	Ella와 나는 방에 있다.
skirt	치마	The pink skirt is Julia's.	그 분홍 치마는 Julia의 것이다.
hill	언덕	I fly my kites on the hill.	나는 언덕에서 나의 연들을 날린다.
dictionary	사전	We buy a new dictionary.	우리는 새 사전을 산다.
scarf	스카프	The scarf is hers.	그 스카프는 그녀의 것이다.
remember	기억하다	We remember you.	우리는 너를 기억한다.
invite	초대하다	He invites our to the party.	그는 우리를 그 파티에 초대한다.

rabbit	토끼	Those rabbits have long ears.	저 토끼들은 긴 귀를 가지고 있다.
famous	유명한	That artist is famous.	저 화가는 유명하다.
expensive	비싼	These tickets are expensive.	이 티켓들은 비싸다.
interesting	재미있는	That is an interesting book.	저것은 재미있는 책이다.
bean	콩	These beans are green.	이 콩들은 녹색이다.
stamp	우표	Those are stamps.	저것들은 우표들이다.
garden	정원	This is a beautiful garden.	이것은 아름다운 정원이다.
hungry	배고픈	Those are hungry horses.	저것들은 배고픈 말들이다.
hairpin	헤어핀	Those hairpins are ours.	저 헤어핀들은 우리들의 것이다.
lily	백합꽃	These flowers are lilies.	이 꽃들은 백합꽃들이다.
spider	거미	That is a big spider.	저것은 큰 거미이다.
sweet	달콤한	Those cookies are very sweet.	저 쿠키들은 매우 달콤하다.
photo	사진	I like these photos.	나는 이 사진들을 좋아한다.
delicious	맛있는	Those apples look delicious.	저 사과들은 맛있어 보인다.
scientist	과학자	She is a scientist.	그녀는 과학자이다.
palace	궁전	That is a big palace.	저것은 큰 궁전이다.
program	프로그램	This program is interesting.	이 프로그램은 재미있다.
glove	장갑	These are red gloves.	이것들은 빨간 장갑들이다.
dirty	더러운	Those clothes are really dirty.	이 옷들은 정말 더럽다.
pumpkin	호박	This is a pumpkin.	이것은 호박이다.
brown	갈색	Those are brown leaves.	저것들은 갈색 잎들이다.
colorful	화려한	Those feathers are colorful.	저 깃털들은 화려하다.
sharp	날카로운	These are sharp knives.	이것들은 날카로운 칼들이다.
classroom	교실	That classroom is dirty.	저 교실은 더럽다.
hotel	호텔	These hotels are expensive.	이 호텔들은 비싸다.
thick	두꺼운	This is a thick book.	이것은 두꺼운 책이다.
cousin	사촌	That is my cousin.	저분은 나의 사촌이다.
cheap	(값) 싼	This watch is cheap.	이 손목시계는 싸다.
castle	성	That is an old castle.	저것은 오래된 성이다.
heavy	무거운	Those bats are heavy.	저 야구 방망이는 무겁다.

difficult	어려운	The question is difficult.	그 문제는 어렵다.
brave	용감한	Ann and Tom are brave.	Ann과 Tom은 용감하다.
genius	천재	The boy is a genius.	그 소년은 천재이다.
enough	충분한	The water is enough.	그 물은 충분하다.
soldier	군인	His brother is a soldier.	그의 형은 군인이다.
high	높은	This building is high.	이 빌딩은 높다.
engineer	기술자	We are engineers.	우리는 기술자들이다.
actress	여배우	She is a famous actress.	그녀는 유명한 여배우이다.
bright	밝은	The stars are bright.	그 별들은 밝다.
ladder	사다리	I am on the ladder.	나는 사다리 위에 있다.
warm	따뜻한	These sweaters are warm.	이 스웨터들은 따뜻하다.
wonderful	훌륭한	The photos are wonderful.	그 사진들은 훌륭하다.
husband	남편	I am her husband.	나는 그녀의 남편이다.
dancer	댄서	Jacob is a dancer.	Jacob은 댄서이다.
musician	음악가	She is a musician.	그녀는 음악가이다.
hairdresser	미용사	My aunt is a hairdresser.	나의 이모는 미용사이다.
full	배부른	Julie and you are full.	Julie와 너는 배가 부르다.
pianist	피아니스트	I am a pianist.	나는 피아니스트이다.
daughter	딸	She is my daughter.	그녀는 나의 딸이다.
astronaut	우주비행사	You are an astronaut.	너는 우주비행사이다.
broken	깨진	The windows are broken.	그 창문은 깨져 있다.
pet	애완동물	Those are their pets.	저것들은 그들의 애완동물들이다.
store	가게	The store is open.	그 가게는 열려 있다.
thief	도둑	That man is a thief.	저 사람은 도둑이다.
fresh	신선한	This carrot is fresh.	이 당근은 신선하다.
raincoat	비옷	It is a raincoat.	그것은 비옷이다.
light	가벼운	These are light stones.	이것들은 가벼운 돌들이다.
carpenter	목수	That carpenter is thirsty.	저 목수는 목이 마르다.
insect	곤충	Those are small insects.	저것들은 작은 곤충들이다.
nephew	조카	You are his nephew.	너는 그의 조카이다.

easy	쉬운	The test is not easy.	그 시험은 쉽지 않다.
boring	지루한	This book is not boring.	이 책은 지루하지 않다.
surprised	놀란	They are not surprised.	그들은 놀라지 않는다.
apartment	아파트	This is our apartment.	이것은 우리의 아파트이다.
fault	잘못	It is not your fault.	그것은 너의 잘못이 아니다.
concert	콘서트	The concert is not good.	그 콘서트는 좋지 않다.
market	시장	Her mother is in the market.	그녀의 어머니는 시장에 있다.
birthday	생일	Is your birthday tomorrow?	너의 생일은 내일이니?
gift	선물	Is that gift for her?	저 선물은 그녀를 위한 거니?
active	활동적인	Are you active?	너는 활동적이니?
quiet	조용한	Are the children quiet?	그 어린이들은 조용하니?
noisy	시끄러운	Is Peter noisy?	Peter는 시끄럽니?
drawer	서랍	My socks are in the drawer.	내 양말은 서랍에 있다.
interested	관심 있는	He is interested in movies.	그는 영화에 관심이 있다.
painting	그림	These paintings are beautiful.	이 그림들은 아름답다.
suit	정장	Is that Brian's suit?	저것은 Brian의 정장이니?
baker	제빵사	Is he a famous baker?	그는 유명한 제빵사니?
lipstick	립스틱	Is this Jenny's lipstick?	이것은 Jenny의 립스틱이니?
lazy	게으른	Is your sister lazy?	너의 여동생은 게으르니?
shy	수줍어하는	Her daughter is shy.	그녀의 딸은 수줍어한다.
exam	시험	This exam is difficult.	이 시험은 어렵다.
giraffe	기린	The giraffes are very tall.	그 기린들은 매우 크다.
inventor	발명가	He is a great inventor.	그는 훌륭한 발명가이다.
farmer	농부	You are a farmer.	너는 농부이다.
job	직업	Your job is interesting.	너의 직업은 재미있다.
dark	어두운	It is dark outside.	밖은 어둡다.
station	역	The station is near here.	그 역은 여기 근처에 있다.
gentle	온순한	Is your horse gentle?	너의 말은 온순하니?
button	단추	Is this a button?	이것은 단추이니?
rich	부유한	Are they rich men?	그들은 부유한 사람들이니?

다음 우리말 뜻에 맞는 영어 단어를 쓰시오.

1　좋은, 착한　_____

2　선생님　_____

3　예쁜　_____

4　키가 큰　_____

5　친절한　_____

6　아름다운　_____

7　나무　_____

8　축구　_____

9　가수　_____

10　숙제　_____

11　경찰관　_____

12　닫다　_____

13　배우다　_____

14　열다　_____

15　의사　_____

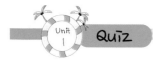

다음 우리말 뜻에 맞는 영어 단어를 쓰시오.

1   걷다   _____

2   바이올린   _____

3   코끼리   _____

4   테니스   _____

5   방   _____

6   저녁 식사   _____

7   상자   _____

8   자전거   _____

9   슬픈   _____

10   열심히   _____

11   탁자   _____

12   영리한   _____

13   여자 형제   _____

14   주스   _____

15   씻다   _____

다음 우리말 뜻에 맞는 영어 단어를 쓰시오.

1 도시 _____

2 사진, 그림 _____

3 사탕 _____

4 손목시계 _____

5 복숭아 _____

6 황소 _____

7 쥐 _____

8 우편배달부 _____

9 교회 _____

10 장미 _____

11 병원 _____

12 첼로 _____

13 지도 _____

14 연 _____

15 라디오 _____

다음 우리말 뜻에 맞는 영어 단어를 쓰시오.

1	벤치	_____
2	어린이	_____
3	지붕	_____
4	치아	_____
5	꽃	_____
6	접시	_____
7	아기	_____
8	여우	_____
9	사과	_____
10	친구	_____
11	나뭇잎	_____
12	드레스	_____
13	사슴	_____
14	건물	_____
15	버스	_____

다음 우리말 뜻에 맞는 영어 단어를 쓰시오.

1	알다	_____
2	마시다	_____
3	비	_____
4	살다	_____
5	잉크	_____
6	빵	_____
7	시간	_____
8	방문하다	_____
9	기름	_____
10	희망	_____
11	사랑	_____
12	원하다	_____
13	햇빛	_____
14	밀가루	_____
15	밥, 쌀	_____

다음 우리말 뜻에 맞는 영어 단어를 쓰시오.

1 고기 _____

2 비누 _____

3 샴푸 _____

4 후추 _____

5 초콜릿 _____

6 샐러드 _____

7 수프 _____

8 우유 _____

9 버터 _____

10 피자 _____

11 치즈 _____

12 포도 _____

13 소금 _____

14 설탕 _____

15 종이 _____

다음 우리말 뜻에 맞는 영어 단어를 쓰시오.

1	도끼	_____
2	양파	_____
3	식사	_____
4	대학	_____
5	닫다	_____
6	달	_____
7	꼬리	_____
8	바이올린	_____
9	매일	_____
10	말하다	_____
11	함께	_____
12	기타	_____
13	나의 것	_____
14	준비가 된	_____
15	서쪽	_____

다음 우리말 뜻에 맞는 영어 단어를 쓰시오.

1 앨범 _____

2 구름 _____

3 배우 _____

4 가져오다 _____

5 중국 _____

6 둥근 _____

7 바다 _____

8 유럽 사람 _____

9 화가 _____

10 천사 _____

11 재킷 _____

12 시험 _____

13 항해하다 _____

14 과목 _____

15 떠오르다 _____

다음 우리말 뜻에 맞는 영어 단어를 쓰시오.

1 쿠키 _____

2 강아지 _____

3 동물 _____

4 늦은 _____

5 쓰다 _____

6 아들 _____

7 수의사 _____

8 짧은 _____

9 표지 _____

10 달리다 _____

11 일찍 _____

12 아픈 _____

13 졸린 _____

14 도서관 _____

15 카메라 _____

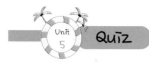
다음 우리말 뜻에 맞는 영어 단어를 쓰시오.

1 피곤한 _____

2 영화 _____

3 근처에 _____

4 서두르다 _____

5 방 _____

6 식당 _____

7 초대하다 _____

8 친한 _____

9 햄스터 _____

10 치마 _____

11 요리사 _____

12 사전 _____

13 스카프 _____

14 기억하다 _____

15 언덕 _____

다음 우리말 뜻에 맞는 영어 단어를 쓰시오.

1 콩 _____

2 유명한 _____

3 정원 _____

4 재미있는 _____

5 토끼 _____

6 우표 _____

7 비싼 _____

8 배고픈 _____

9 사진 _____

10 백합꽃 _____

11 거미 _____

12 달콤한 _____

13 헤어핀 _____

14 맛있는 _____

15 과학자 _____

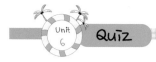
다음 우리말 뜻에 맞는 영어 단어를 쓰시오.

1 호박 _____

2 프로그램 _____

3 장갑 _____

4 더러운 _____

5 궁전 _____

6 갈색 _____

7 (값) 싼 _____

8 날카로운 _____

9 교실 _____

10 호텔 _____

11 화려한 _____

12 사촌 _____

13 두꺼운 _____

14 성 _____

15 무거운 _____

다음 우리말 뜻에 맞는 영어 단어를 쓰시오.

1 아픈 _____

2 친한 _____

3 긴 _____

4 문제 _____

5 어려운 _____

6 화난 _____

7 높은 _____

8 바쁜 _____

9 무거운 _____

10 배고픈 _____

11 천재 _____

12 충분한 _____

13 텔레비전 _____

14 군인 _____

15 용감한 _____

다음 우리말 뜻에 맞는 영어 단어를 쓰시오.

1	축구 선수	_____
2	여배우	_____
3	미용사	_____
4	사다리	_____
5	남편	_____
6	훌륭한	_____
7	따뜻한	_____
8	댄서	_____
9	밝은	_____
10	미국인	_____
11	만화책	_____
12	음악가	_____
13	모든 사람	_____
14	배부른	_____
15	기술자	_____

다음 우리말 뜻에 맞는 영어 단어를 쓰시오.

1	조용한	_____
2	일본	_____
3	쉬운	_____
4	놀란	_____
5	콘서트	_____
6	잘못	_____
7	아파트	_____
8	시장	_____
9	어두운	_____
10	생일	_____
11	활동적인	_____
12	선물	_____
13	단추	_____
14	곤충	_____
15	지루한	_____

다음 우리말 뜻에 맞는 영어 단어를 쓰시오.

1	은행	_____
2	배낭	_____
3	그림	_____
4	관심 있는	_____
5	게으른	_____
6	축구공	_____
7	기린	_____
8	정장	_____
9	시끄러운	_____
10	립스틱	_____
11	영화	_____
12	수줍어하는	_____
13	제빵사	_____
14	시험	_____
15	서랍	_____

Answer Key

Unit 1 | Quiz 1회
p. 10

1 good 2 teacher 3 pretty 4 tall 5 kind
6 beautiful 7 tree 8 soccer 9 singer
10 homework 11 police officer 12 close
13 learn 14 open 15 doctor

Unit 1 | Quiz 2회
p. 11

1 walk 2 violin 3 elephant 4 tennis
5 room 6 dinner 7 box 8 bike 9 sad
10 hard 11 table 12 smart 13 sister
14 juice 15 wash

Unit 2 | Quiz 1회
p. 12

1 city 2 picture 3 candy 4 watch
5 peach 6 ox 7 mouse 8 mailman
9 church 10 rose 11 hospital 12 cello
13 map 14 kite 15 radio

Unit 2 | Quiz 2회
p. 13

1 bench 2 child 3 roof 4 tooth 5 flower
6 dish 7 baby 8 fox 9 apple 10 friend
11 leaf 12 dress 13 deer 14 building
15 bus

Unit 3 | Quiz 1회
p. 14

1 know 2 drink 3 rain 4 live 5 ink
6 bread 7 time 8 visit 9 oil 10 hope
11 love 12 want 13 sunshine 14 flour
15 rice

Unit 3 | Quiz 2회
p. 15

1 meat 2 soap 3 shampoo 4 pepper
5 chocolate 6 salad 7 soup 8 milk
9 butter 10 pizza 11 cheese 12 grape
13 salt 14 sugar 15 paper

Unit 4 | Quiz 1회
p. 16

1 ax 2 onion 3 meal 4 university
5 close 6 moon 7 tail 8 violin
9 everyday 10 speak 11 together
12 guitar 13 mine 14 ready 15 west

Unit 4 | Quiz 2회
p. 17

1 album 2 cloud 3 actor 4 bring
5 China 6 round 7 sea 8 European
9 artist 10 angel 11 jacket 12 test
13 sail 14 subject 15 rise

Memo

초등 영어 교재의 베스트셀러

초등 영어 문법 실력 쌓기!

Grammar Builder 1

Grammar Builder 시리즈

You Are the Only One!

Words in Grammar

Iam books

초등 영어 문법 실력 쌓기!

Grammar Builder

1

Words in Grammar

You Are the Only One!

Iam books